KU-638-180

Contents

PART I
WISDOM OF THE ELDERS

PART II
STORYTELLING AND INDIGENOUS PEDAGOGIES FOR BUSINESS ETHICS

PART III
TRADE, BARTER, AND ETHICAL BUSINESS RELATIONSHIPS

TRIBAL WISDOM FOR BUSINESS ETHICS

BY

GRACE ANN ROSILE

*New Mexico State University, Las Cruces,
New Mexico, USA*

UNIVERSITY OF WINCHESTER
LIBRARY

Emerald

United Kingdom – North America – Japan
India – Malaysia – China

Emerald Group Publishing Limited
Howard House, Wagon Lane, Bingley BD16 1WA, UK

First edition 2016

Copyright © 2016 Emerald Group Publishing Limited

Reprints and permissions service
Contact: permissions@emeraldinsight.com

No part of this book may be reproduced, stored in a retrieval system, transmitted
in any form or by any means electronic, mechanical, photocopying, recording or
otherwise without either the prior written permission of the publisher or a licence
permitting restricted copying issued in the UK by The Copyright Licensing Agency
and in the USA by The Copyright Clearance Center. Any opinions expressed in the
chapters are those of the authors. Whilst Emerald makes every effort to ensure the
quality and accuracy of its content, Emerald makes no representation implied or
otherwise, as to the chapters' suitability and application and disclaims any
warranties, express or implied, to their use.

British Library Cataloguing in Publication Data
A catalogue record for this book is available from the British Library

ISBN: 978-1-78635-288-0

Printed and bound by CPI Group (UK) Ltd, Croydon, CR0 4YY

UNIVERSITY OF WINCHESTER

ISOQAR certified
Management System,
awarded to Emerald
for adherence to
Environmental
standard
ISO 14001:2004.

ISOQAR
REGISTERED
Certificate Number 1985
ISO 14001

INVESTOR IN PEOPLE

List of Figures

Chapter 14

Chapter 15

List of Cases

List of Contributors

Calvin M. Boardman	University of Utah, Salt Lake City, UT, USA
David M. Boje	New Mexico State University, Las Cruces, NM, USA
Gregory Cajete	University of New Mexico, Albuquerque, NM, USA
Carma M. Claw	New Mexico State University, Las Cruces, NM, USA
Lisa Grayshield	New Mexico State University, Las Cruces, NM, USA
Maria Humphries	University of Waikato, Hamilton, New Zealand
Deanna M. Kennedy	University of Washington Bothell, Bothell, WA, USA
Matthew Kolan	University of Vermont, Burlington, VT, USA
Gerri Elise McCulloh	New Mexico State University, Las Cruces, NM, USA
Vincent J. Pascal	Eastern Washington University, Spokane, WA, USA

Donald D. Pepion	New Mexico State University, Las Cruces, NM, USA
Grace Ann Rosile	New Mexico State University, Las Cruces, NM, USA
Mabel Sanchez	New Mexico State University, Las Cruces, NM, USA
Daniel Stewart	Gonzaga University, Spokane, WA, USA
Kaylynn Sullivan TwoTrees	University of Vermont, Burlington, VT, USA
Amy Klemm Verbos	University of Wisconsin-Whitewater, Whitewater, WI, USA

I dedicate this book to my husband David M. Boje,
who brought love and adventure to my life,
and helped me find my voice as a writer.

Preface and Map to the Territory

I am Grace Ann Rosile, Ph.D., Professor of Management at New Mexico State University. My family is from the Western Pennsylvania area around Pittsburgh. I am of Italian-American heritage, or, as I sometime say, half Italian and half Sicilian. Those distinctions used to be important to some people, like those who wanted to know from what village in Sicily my maternal grandfather came (San Filipo). During my many years in graduate school, that same grandfather was highly skeptical. I must not be working like I should, to take so long, and then not even be a "real" doctor!

Overview: This book is an outgrowth of several years of filmmaking, plus a two-day conference, on Tribal Wisdom for Business Ethics. Beginning in 2010, I headed up a project which two years later produced a 28-minute educational film called *Tribal Wisdom for Business Ethics*. Released in 2012, the focus in the film was on the eight Aspects:

Eight Aspects of Tribal Wisdom

1. **Relationships** are an end in themselves
2. **Gifting** is valued more highly
3. **Egalitarianism** is preferred

4. **Non-acquisitiveness** is valued not greed

5. **Usefulness** or access to use is valued

6. **Barter** for what is needed

7. **Trust** and Buyer Trust are valued

8. **Disclosure** is full and voluntary

Films: Then in 2013, I and my group of collaborators produced six shorter films:

1. Tribal Wisdom and Marketing Strategy;

2. Tribal Wisdom and Indigenous Ways of Knowing;

3. Indigenous Trading, Disclosure, and Barter;

4. Tribal Wisdom and Storytelling;

5. Tribal Wisdom and Entrepreneurship; and

6. Tribal Wisdom for Life-Enhancing Relationships.

In the process of interviewing the experts featured in the film, all expressed an interest in participating in a future conference on Tribal Wisdom.

Conference: Everyone was invited to New Mexico State University (NMSU) in Las Cruces, NM to share ideas. From those beginnings, we have this collaborative written work. This book allows us to go into more depth on particular topics. Also, we offer some frameworks to put these ideas into a coherent integrated approach for framing a mutually beneficial conversation between "Tribal Wisdom" and business ethics.

Tribal Relevance: Why should tribal people be interested in this book? First, we expect it will be reassuring for tribal people to see that the Euro-western business world shows indications of moving in directions more compatible with their traditional values and beliefs. This book might offer hope to some who think they will have to give up traditional values, perhaps their very identity, to succeed in the non-tribal business world. We see the initial stages of development of a business community where tribal people would feel at home.

Second, as these values and practices are gathered from a variety of sources, this book offers a rare collection of traditional tribal wisdoms that have huge potential relevance for a business context. Finally, both tribal and non-tribal peoples will gain a greater understanding and appreciation of how business has been able to contribute to stronger communities with stronger relationships.

Co-Created Benefits: Each chapter in this book contributes to co-creating our collective vision. In this vision, businesses gain a better understanding of how tribal values and practices already have been introduced into the Euro-western business world. These values and practices can be developed further and used more widely for an increasingly ethical kind of success. At the same time, tribal peoples can be encouraged by the heightened awareness of how doing business "their way" may be compatible with, and may even be a key to their own success in the non-indigenous world.

It is my hope that we come to see ourselves not as "sides," as indigenous or non-indigenous. Rather, we are travelers on the same road, each seeking socially, spiritually, and economically sustainable paths through the world, paths which will nourish our unique cultures while fostering mutual benefit for all.

Map to the Territory: This book contains 19 chapters, many of which have embedded case examples and activities. There are also stand-alone case examples, questions, and activities. At the end of each chapter, you will see some "Search for Wisdom" questions, accompanied by a feather icon:

Search for Wisdom

You will see "Grace Ann's Note" in a shadowed box to indicate that I am speaking, as follows:

Grace Ann's Note

The chapters are divided into four parts. Part I is "Wisdom of the Elders." This section provides an orientation to Tribal Wisdom, indigenous ways-of-knowing, indigenous perspectives on the natural environment in relationship to humans and the business world, and a general orientation to business ethics.

In Chapter 1, I begin our journey by introducing the "eight aspects" of Tribal Wisdom. These concepts were identified in the previous work on Tribal Wisdom (described above) which was the impetus for the present volume. In addition to these eight core concepts, this chapter offers three reasons why Tribal Wisdom concepts might be insightfully applied to contemporary businesses.

In Chapter 2, Dr. Donald Pepion lets us inside some of his own personal journey to his position as a respected elder in his tribe. He describes how he sought wisdom from his elders. Currently, he passes on that wisdom both in the tribal community and through his extensive history of many important roles in university settings. In Chapter 3, Dr. Lisa Grayshield provides us with some enlightening quotes about indigenous ways-of-knowing and Euro-Western science. She discusses the sustainability implications for businesses.

In Chapter 4, Dr. Gregory Cajete contributes aspects of his long stream of environmentally oriented research. He discusses why ethics in business must address environmental issues. He explains how nature, in the principle of mutual reciprocal behavior, can guide us in understanding how we can live lives that are more ethical and sustainable. The Acoma Case concludes this chapter.

I end this first part of the book by placing Tribal Wisdom within a context of the recent trends in business ethics literature in Chapter 5. It is apparent that this literature is moving towards more relational and group-oriented concepts of ethics. Thus, the field is heading in the direction already visible in tribal values. Part I concludes with the case of the NOVA Corporation written by Mabel Sanchez. You are invited to "Search for Wisdom" by considering the questions at the end of the case.

Part II is entitled "Storytelling and Indigenous Pedagogies for Business Ethics." Here, we explore storytelling as a preferred indigenous way of conveying cultural information. Chapter 6 begins the section with a transcription of "A Coyote Story" as told by Dr. Gregory Cajete to Tribal Wisdom filmmakers in 2011.

In Chapter 7, Dr. David M. Boje explains the important differences between indigenous storytelling, traditional Euro-western storytelling, and what his theory calls "Living Story." He uses the concept of "antenarrative" to demonstrate the differences in these storytelling methodologies. In Chapter 8, I reappear to explain some of the particular ways tribes use storytelling to convey ethical principles. We conclude this section with a "Search for Wisdom" with several short example questions.

Now that we have set the stage with indigenous ways-of-knowing, eight Aspects of Tribal Wisdom, business ethics in general, and how these concepts are conveyed through story, Part III digs into more specific business practices, case examples, and ethical teachings. Part III begins with the case example of Dardan Enterprises, written by one of the co-founders of the company, Dr. Daniel Stewart. Next, Chapter 10 discusses "Native American Values Applied to Leadership and Business Ethics Education." Here, Amy Klemm Verbos, Deanna M. Kennedy, and Carma M. Claw, three American Indian professors teaching in colleges of business, offer their views on how ethical values and principles were taught to them, from their various tribal traditions.

In Chapter 11, Dr. Calvin M. Boardman explains the different cultural roots and assumptions that led to different styles of trade among early tribes, even before contact with Euro-Westerners during colonization. He finds reasons for misunderstandings and conflicts in these different trading practices. He also sees hope for greater understanding as we move forward in finding more mutually beneficial ways of conducting business between the indigenous world and the Euro-Western one.

In Chapter 12, I return to discuss the need for equal power relationships, viewed from a storytelling perspective. "Power Stories and Mutually Beneficial Negotiations: Fostering Ensemble Leadership" demonstrates the disempowering potential of even desires to be helpful, when the situation is perceived as one of unequal power. The chapter concludes with a new theory of "Ensemble Leadership" whose roots go back to ancient Mesoamerican cultures.

We conclude Part III with another case from Drs. Daniel Stewart and Vincent J. Pascal. This concluding case is a hypothetical example based on some real-life dynamics of doing business to benefit a company's home community. The case, "Native American Entrepreneurship: Locating Your Business," asks you where you would locate a business: closer to its potential market, or closer to its potential employees, when those two groups are considerable distances apart.

Part IV focuses on Tribal Wisdom insights into businesses in partnership with the natural environment. I introduce this section with a short case example of the experience of our cover artist Virginia Maria Romero. In "Remember to Remember: The Alameda Transit Station," I recall the words of Dr. Gregory Cajete about the importance of remembering our connection to the natural world, as we are nature ourselves.

Dr. David M. Boje provides a penetrating critique of how the "Triple Bottom Line" of people, profit, and planet may not live up to its promise, in Chapter 15. In Chapter 16, Dr. Gerri Elise

McCulloh gives a personal account of growing up on the fringes of Bighorn Medicine Wheel, and experiencing firsthand the dilemma of protecting a natural environmental treasure and sacred site, while allowing appropriate access and appreciation of it.

Bringing these lessons home to our own relationships, Kaylynn Sullivan TwoTrees and Matthew Kolan offer the insightful Chapter 17, "The Trees Are Breathing Us: An Indigenous View of Relationship in Nature and Business." After reading this chapter, you will understand relationships in a whole new way.

Concluding the volume, Dr. Maria Humphries draws parallels between this book and her extensive experience with the Maori indigenous peoples of New Zealand. She fearlessly addresses the topic of what a non-indigenous female can contribute to this discussion. As an outsider living and studying indigenous cultures from both a critical theory perspective and an environmental perspective, she offers her personal views on bridging the indigenous/non-indigenous divide, in mutually beneficial ways.

Finally, we follow Dr. Gregory Cajete's advice in earlier chapters, about giving more "hints" as to the meaning of our morality tales than was traditionally done in tribes. So if you read this whole book, I promise not to leave you wondering. I offer suggested answers to some puzzling questions raised (mostly in Chapter 8), in the "Epilogue".

Free Materials: The Tribal Wisdom films that are part of the genesis of this book are complementary to, but not a replacement for, this volume. There are many points of connection between this book and the films, but very little repetition. All films, plus supporting teaching materials, were created through a grant from the NMSU Daniels Fund Ethics Initiative, and are available for free on the internet at:

http://business.nmsu.edu/research/programs/daniels-ethics/tribal-ethics/.

Thanks: We offer heartfelt thanks to the New Mexico State University Daniels Fund Ethics Initiative, which funded the early work on developing Tribal Wisdom ethics education materials beginning in 2010. They funded the educational filmmaking through 2013, and then in September of 2013 funded the Tribal Wisdom Conference. We are grateful for the many talented and articulate people who participated in the Tribal Wisdom project over the years.

Scholarships: To show appreciation for the all the indigenous scholars and business persons who participated, and to the Daniels Fund Ethics Initiative at NMSU, proceeds from this book will go to a fund for scholarships for American Indian students at NMSU. To contribute, contact the NMSU Foundation office by calling (800) 342-6678 or (575) 646-6126 during business hours. You can also search the web page at https://advancing.nmsu.edu/givenow or e-mail the office at giftacct@nmsu.edu.

Intention: My intention with this work is to encourage mutually respectful relationships. This intention finds expression in the words attributed to Lilla Watson, Gangulu woman, and Murri visual artist:

> "If you have come here to help me, you are wasting our time. But if you have come because your liberation is tied up with mine, then let us work together".

Watson herself prefers that the quote be attributed to "Aboriginal activists group, Queensland, 1970s." It is my hope that this book helps readers to understand and appreciate themselves as well as others more fully so that we may all enjoy more harmonious relationships.

Grace Ann Rosile
Editor

Part I
Wisdom of the Elders

Eight Aspects of Tribal Wisdom for Business Ethics, and Why They Matter

Grace Ann Rosile with cases by Carma M. Claw

Contexts — Traditional Native American Indian tribal cultures reflect a variety of differences from the Euro-Western American cultures. While both cultures engage in "business" as economic trade and negotiations, each comes from different social contexts. It is valuable for each tradition to learn about the nature of the other, as such cross-cultural explorations lead to a better understanding of one's own culture in comparison to an "other." These comparisons are most helpful when each side can discover, adapt, and adopt new ways of dealing with common challenges. Also, each culture offers a different story about how certain values and practices can play out over time.

Cross-Cultural — In this book, we offer a cross-cultural view, and a story of how some Native American Indian tribal traditions and practices can lead to a different way of doing business, both within and across cultural boundaries. These differences are often more a matter of emphasis rather than harsh divergences. Most differences we address are cases of more/less emphasis, not a sharp absence/presence distinction.

Resonances — If we work to find the resonances between tribal wisdoms and Euro-Western business practices, we contribute to the bridge between these different cultures. One important caution to the reader: We can never understand another's culture the way the other does, just as we can never truly understand another's experience except in a mediated, approximate way. Knowing this, we may yet benefit from this admittedly limited ability to experience and understand the "other," those who are unlike the self in some way.

Alligators — There is a humorous story about a tourist in Florida. She admired the necklace worn by a local Indian, and asked what it was made of. The Indian said: "Alligator's teeth." Fingering her own necklace of costly real pearls, she said somewhat patronizingly "I suppose that they mean as much to you as pearls do to us." "Oh no," the Indian objected. "Anyone can open an oyster."

We want to keep in mind that this cross-cultural venture is, as Dr. Don Pepion notes elsewhere in this volume, "a precarious journey." We want to remain humble, recognizing the inherent limitations in this cross-cultural effort. As Pepion reminded us, "Native and academic scholars must be attuned to ethical boundaries and trust in the process of how cultures create truth."

Guideposts — In this book, we cite similar trends and resonances in ethics, leadership, and organization, to help us anchor our understandings of each other's cultures in some perceived similarities. This does not mean that these similar features are "just like" something we know, and now we have our finger on "the" meanings we seek. Rather, these are a starting point, guideposts along the way, to give us glimmers of our goal of better understanding, each of the other.

Self-Awareness — As we are able to experience the other, in admittedly limited ways, we may see and understand ourselves better. This better understanding of self also allows for greater possibilities for change, and more informed choices about the nature and direction of change. From such a position, we will have greater potential for more ethical inclusiveness, for more mutual influence, for more of Boje's cocreated storying, for the mutual advantage of all.

Eight Aspects of Tribal Wisdom and Relevance for Business Ethics

We have chosen eight values and practices commonly found in tribal indigenous cultures which are most relevant to the conduct of business. While there are by some estimates over 500 such tribal cultures among Native American Indians alone, and there may be more differences than similarities among these various tribes, yet there are some common elements. These common themes are drawn from a variety of tribal cultures, and are common to most American Indian tribes. We focus on the similarities which we perceive from studying indigenous and non-indigenous scholars,

Table 1.1: Eight Aspects of Tribal Wisdom versus Euro-Western Business Values and Practices.

Eight Aspects of Tribal Wisdom	Euro-Western Values/Practices
1. *Relationships* are an end in themselves	Relationships are a means to an end
2. *Gifting* is valued more highly	Getting/acquiring is valued
3. *Egalitarianism* is preferred	Hierarchy is preferred
4. *Non-acquisitiveness* is valued not greed	Accumulation of wealth
5. *Usefulness* or access to use is valued	Ownership is most valued
6. *Barter* for what is needed	Acquire according to supply/demand
7. *Trust* and Buyer Trust are valued	Buyer Beware still exists
8. *Disclosure* is full and voluntary	Truth to the extent required by law

Note: The Eight Aspects discussed in the above table are excerpted and modified slightly from Rosile (2014), IACCM Conference Proceedings.

as well as our own interviews and films reflecting the insights of indigenous and non-indigenous business practitioners.

The following eight aspects of traditional tribal values and practices have special applicability for business ethics. The eight aspects of Tribal Wisdom are presented in a numbered list. However, the reader is cautioned to remember that these eight items are called "aspects," and not "laws" or "commandments" or even "dominant norms." They are numbered only for organizational purposes for non-indigenous minds. The eight aspects could be best thought of as a hologram, where each part contains the whole. In fact, for some indigenous experts, it was difficult to separate one aspect from another, since all are so closely interrelated around the concept of "relationship."

1. **Relationship**

   Relationship is a key value in American Indian cultures. The other aspects of tribal values discussed here may all be interpreted as aspects of, or contributors to, the primary value of relationship. Further, relationship refers not only to social relations, but also to human relations with the natural environment, and with the universe of all that is.

   This sense of relatedness also influences what is perceived as fair. When trading parties had close social relationships, then the profits earned from those close trading partners were expected to be reduced (Wilmoth, 2006). This same type of dynamic might occur today. If we were selling our used car to a favorite brother or sister, we might want to give them a much better selling price than if we sold to a stranger. Similarly, a business transaction is greatly affected by social relationships in indigenous cultures. Specifically, business profits are secondary to, and supportive of, social relationships within the family and tribe.

   Conversely, in the Euro-Western business context, the phrase "Business is business" implies that business profit is at best unrelated to, or in the worst case, takes precedence over, social relationships (Korten, 1995). The Euro-Western world often views humans, plants, and animals as means to an end, as resources to be employed in the making of profits. In contrast, indigenous cultures view business as a means to the end of enhancing a harmonious balance of relationships among humans and the planet (Cordova, 2007; and many others).

Having and showing respect is one way tribal cultures build good relationships. Respect is the external sign of that relationship. When relationships are out of balance, then ceremony is how balance and harmony is restored. For example, when harvesting plant or animal food, tribal traditions employ ceremonies to give thanks for the food and restore the balance between humans and planet.

2. **Gifting Rather than Getting**
   Euro-Western business philosophy often endorses the "Greed is Good" philosophy. In contrast, American Indian cultures explicitly value giving more than getting. A person who gives back to the community earns more respect than one who makes a profit from the community. This does not mean that profit is avoided or disdained. It is simply less important than generosity (Harris, 2000; Rosile & Boardman, 2011; and many others).

   Rosile, Pepion, Boje, and Gladstone (2012) reports that Blackfeet hunters would share their buffalo with older, weaker, or otherwise needy people of the tribe. Gladstone (2012) agrees that sharing was expected within tribes, and still is today, even though the dominant culture promotes greed and personal wealth. As an example, Gladstone (2012) cites the *give-away* or *potlatch*. These traditions return wealth to the community, both as a form of giving thanks, and as a tithe on personal earned wealth.

3. **Egalitarianism versus Hierarchy**
   In the Euro-Western system, business is often viewed as similar to warfare, is described in the language of war or competitive sports, and is the arena where one proves one's superiority to others. American Indians have tribal indigenous cultures, where by definition the tribe is more important

than the individual. This tribal orientation in American Indian cultures expresses itself in the desire for egalitarianism (Rosile & Boardman, 2011). Pepion (in Rosile, Pepion, & Gladstone, 2012) notes that "many tribes use verbal shaming of any individual who gives the appearance of being better than others ... ."

4. **Non-Acquisitiveness**
   Euro-Western capitalism is rooted in the idea of accumulation of wealth as a good and desired end. American Indians tend to view such accumulation as a community-eroding greed. Instead, taking only what one needs is valued as a way to assure that all have enough (Alicia Ortega, interview in film *Tribal Wisdom for Business Ethics*, 2014; Rosile & Boardman, 2011.)

5. **Usefulness**
   Following from the desire for non-acquisitiveness is the other side of the coin: usefulness. If I need a car, but only one day a week, perhaps I could share a vehicle rather than acquiring one of my own. What is important in traditional tribal values is not so much the ownership as the access to, or use of, something (Boardman, 2010; Rosile & Boardman, 2011).

6. **Barter**
   A barter economy is compatible with a non-acquisitive, use-oriented culture, while a monetary economy more easily accommodates accumulation of wealth (Boardman, 2010; Rosile & Boardman, 2011).

7. **Trust**
   Trust is a key factor in building egalitarian relationships in any culture. In American Indian cultures, the importance of trust carries over to business practices that emphasize keeping one's word, being honest, and following through on commitments (Boardman, 2010; Rosile & Boardman, 2011).

8. **Disclosure**
   The buyer-beware social norm in Euro-Western business culture is still in the process of being dismantled by law-makers and consumer-advocacy groups. In contrast, the

historical practice in traditional American Indian trading was a seller-initiated voluntary full disclosure of the flaws and shortcomings of any item in trade (Jaime Geronimo Vela, interview in the 2013 film *Tribal Wisdom for Business Ethics*; Boardman, 2010; Rosile & Boardman, 2011). Such disclosure practices enhance trust and egalitarianism.

Table 1.1 summarizes and compares these eight aspects of American Indian business-related traditional values and practices, in contrast to Euro-Western values and practices. Here again, we caution that these are broad generalizations, not for limiting or labeling but intended as heuristics for developing greater understanding.

Three Reasons for Applying Tribal Wisdom to Business Ethics

Reason #1: Master Traders — Why should business people be interested in traditional tribal values and practices? There are at least three good reasons. First, tribes in the Americas have a much longer history, a pre-European-contact history, during which they were master traders. They established cross-continental trading routes north and south as well as coast to coast. Their trading relationships flourished for hundreds of years, as shown by evidence such as abalone shell items from the Pacific Northwest found at archeological sites in today's Midwest. Even grade school children are learning about this long-overlooked aspect of our American Indian history. (See the state of Montana's middle school teaching module by Wilmoth, 2006, at http://mhs.mt.gov/Portals/11/education/docs/IEFA LessonPlanTradeBarter.pdf.)

Reason #2: Global Village — Second, tribal traditions may be more relevant to today's business environment than in the past few hundred years. Due to technology of telephone and Internet, our world has shrunk to what some call the "global village." Therefore, the village-type dynamics of concern for maintaining respectful and honest relationships socially and with trading partners is again very relevant in today's global economy.

Reason #3: Wealth Redefined — A third reason to seek business insights from indigenous peoples is to experience a broader definition of wealth, beyond just money. We have heard tribal people rejecting (and rightly so, we think) the Euro-Western label of "poor." They will point out that while they may not be wealthy in dollars, they are rich in tradition, art, culture, family and community ties, relationship with Mother Earth, and spirituality, to name just a few alternative measures of wealth. This reminds me (Grace Ann) of my grandfather, a hard-working immigrant from Italy whose seven children were born in the United States. He had a photo taken inside an unused bank vault with his children around him, because he always referred to his seven children as his seven millions.

Broader definitions of wealth, and especially of profit, already are beginning to have a foothold in corporate America. With the "Triple Bottom Line," corporations are measuring social and environmental impacts by including not just profit, but also planet and people in the balance sheet. The direction of the "Triple Bottom Line" is praise worthy, yet its application leaves much to be desired. This is discussed elsewhere in this volume by Boje.

It is our hope that this book will contribute to a greater appreciation by each culture for the other. Such appreciation is the first step leading to the mutual benefit of all. Appreciation is the first step to even greater commitment by both cultures to the values we hold in common. Mutual appreciation opens the door to even greater dedication to the higher ethical standards to which we all aspire.

Grace Ann's Note

Chapter 1 offered the Eight Aspects of Tribal Wisdom: (1) Relationship; (2) Gifting; (3) Egalitarianism; (4) Non-Acquisitiveness; (5) Usefulness; (6) Barter; (7) Trust; (8) Disclosure. The first aspect, Relationship, is the foundation underlying each aspect. Relationships should be respectful, and reflect balance and harmony. When relationships are disrupted, Ceremony is used to restore balance and harmony.

In the next section, we invite you to "Search for Wisdom" regarding relationships in the following stories. These stories describe situations where language is used to foster respectful relationships and cooperation, in both personal and work life.

Search for Wisdom

— Dr. Grace Ann Rosile

As you read the following stories, search for your own answers to the questions below about the first of the Eight Aspects of Tribal Wisdom: Respect.

1. Can you give some examples of how respect is shown in the way we address others in the workplace?

2. Can you think of examples you have seen of how disrespect was shown in the way someone was addressed in the workplace?

3. Can you suggest some ways to permit and encourage people to appropriately question rules and challenge authority, yet still remain respectful? (Hint: consider whistleblowers who try to reveal wrongdoing of those in authority. How can we support such individuals without disrupting a culture of respect?)

4. In the final story (below) about basketball playoffs, what, if any, sort of "advantage" did the Navajo players have due to their use of the Navajo language?

5. If the Navajo players' use of the Navajo language was an advantage, was in an "unfair" advantage? Why or why not?

CASE VIGNETTE

The Role of Language in Maintaining Relationships and Respect

— *Carma M. Claw*

"Yaazh (son), will you please move the crates away from the door?" A new work day has started in Indian country. Like many Native American communities, Navajos rely heavily on relational ties to address one another, and in a workplace on the reservation, this cultural aspect occurs in every day interactions among employees.

One female warehouse manager instructs a younger employee to help move crates, and she does so by using the kinship form of address, *yaazh*, which means son or nephew. She noticed the increase in cooperation, response time, and the overall disposition of coworkers if she addressed them using traditional Navajo kinship relations using the Navajo language.

In Navajo, relations are based on a clan system; every Navajo has four clans. The first is the mother's clan, the second, the father's, and the third and fourth are the maternal and paternal grandfather clans respectively. Hence, if a person is any of these clans, they are related to you in the same way you would refer to your mother, father, etc. In this instance, the warehouse manager was the same clan as the employee's mother, and so forth.

In this story, the kinship term "Yaazh" does not have a direct translation. It could mean either son or nephew, as it refers to either relative within the same clan. Similarly, the son/nephew might call someone "mother" when the woman is their mother's sister, or even at the initial encounter with someone having the same clan as their mother. The term "auntie" is different for the mother and father's side of the clan. All this reflects close family ties and a broader, more encompassing view of "immediate family" than is typical in the United States.

When, on several occasions, the female warehouse manager failed to use those traditional terms of Navajo kinship, the employees made sure she knew they were displeased. Indeed, even when the "equivalent" English translation, "nephew" was used, they did not like that either. They clearly preferred that the Navajo kinship terms be used when this Navajo manager addressed them in the workplace.

There was an unexpected consequence of using these Navajo forms of address. A non-native coworker felt left out when he learned about the "titles" and relationships. The solution? He was also given a Navajo "title" and adopted into the "family."

Grace Ann's Note

How many words do we have in contemporary US culture that convey honor and respect for elders? Or convey love and appreciation for our young ones?

In contrast, consider this story of Aileen Cruz, a holder of the Miss Native New Mexico State University title, and President of the Native American Business Students Association on campus. Ms. Cruz was interviewed in the film *Tribal Wisdom for Business Ethics*. She is from the Ohkay Owingeh tribe. In the film, she speaks a greeting in her native language which would be used when addressing an elder. She translates this greeting as "With respect, may I have your permission to speak to you?"

These stories by Carma M. Claw and Aileen Cruz demonstrate the role of language in conveying respect in relationships. The language itself, and the way we use our language, influences our relationships and our propensity to work together cooperatively, whether in places of business or in our homes. The next story, also by Carma M. Claw, shows that language can affect not only hierarchical relationships, but also more egalitarian teamwork relationships.

CASE VIGNETTE

Basketball Playoffs

— Carma M. Claw

The crowd is on their feet and cheering. It is state playoffs and this game is a very close one. It's not the first time this Indian reservation high school basketball team is in the playoffs. It's also not the first time they hear degrading and hateful remarks. But, they have their "game faces" on and they push forward.

They call their plays and speak to each other in their Native tongue like they have been all season. The language seemed to bring the team closer together over the years, and it wasn't any different this year. The team encouraged each other using single words in Navajo that had deeper and/or multiple meanings compared to English words, and there are usually not direct translations. For instance, when saying, "watch out," "be careful," or "stop that player," the same one-word phrase can be used, but, the context, in this case, at different times during the game, in which it is used determines what is actually conveyed. They also found ways to tell each other to ignore or laugh-off the sometimes unwelcoming environment. Even when a different tribe or non-Native was part of the team, they learned some of the basic terms and the way they were used.

In some ways it was not a surprise for the referees to halt the game and call the team captains for a discussion. The Indian basketball team was directed to cease using Native language on the court; the reason: it was an unfair advantage. It was the late 1980s and there was no social media to bring attention to this appalling action. Similar actions still occur today such as the Navajo basketball team in Arizona being banned from wearing their traditional Navajo hair buns (Fonseca, 2016).

Search for Wisdom

—Dr. Grace Ann Rosile

After reading these stories, you may "Search for Wisdom" by considering how you might answer the questions below (which also appeared at the start of this section):

1. Can you give some examples of how respect is shown in the way we address others in the workplace?

2. Can you think of examples you have seen of how disrespect was shown in the way someone was addressed in the workplace?

3. Can you suggest some ways to permit and encourage people to appropriately question rules and challenge authority, yet still remain respectful? (Hint: consider whistleblowers who try to reveal wrongdoing of those in authority. How can we support such individuals without disrupting a culture of respect?)

4. In the final story (above) about basketball playoffs, what, if any, sort of "advantage" did the Navajo players have due to their use of the Navajo language?

5. If the Navajo players' use of the Navajo language was an advantage, was in an "unfair" advantage? Why or why not?

Grace Ann's Note

Many thanks to Carma M. Claw for her wonderful stories about language and the power of words to affect our relationships and create a culture of respect and cooperation!

In the next chapter, Dr. Don Pepion provides a personal account of his journey in understanding traditional tribal ways. He connects his experience of indigenous ways-of-knowing with contemporary theories of quantum storytelling. He cautions us that not everything can be known, nor should be told, to outsiders. He warns of the historical tendencies to appropriate and exploit indigenous knowledge, and reminds us of our ethical obligations to respect other cultures.

References

Boardman, C. (2010). Personal interviews, June and October, cal.boardman@utah.edu.

Cordova, V. F. (2007). Against the singularity of the human species. In K. D. Moore, K. Peters, T. Jojola, & A. Lacy (Eds.). *How it is: The Native American philosophy of V. F. Cordova* (pp. 159–165). Tucson, AZ: University of Arizona Press.

Fonseca, F. (2016, Feb. 5). Referee barring Native American hair buns in basketball game causes uproar. *The Arizona Republic*. Associated Press. Retrieved from http://www.azcentral.com/story/news/local/arizona/2016/02/05/call-over-native-american-hair-bun-at-game-prompts-outcry/79860794/

Gladstone, J. S. (2012). *Old Man and Coyote barter: An inquiry into the spirit of a Native American philosophy of business* (Order No. 3537767, New Mexico State University). ProQuest Dissertations and Theses, 284.

Harris, L. (2000). *LaDonna Harris: A comanche life*. Lincoln, NE: University of Nebraska Press.

Korten, D. C. (1995). *When corporations rule the world*. San Francisco, CA: Berrett-Koehler Publishers.

Rosile, G. A. (2014). American Indian Tribal Wisdom: A storytelling model for cross-paradigm business ethics. In *Proceedings of the international association of cross-cultural communication in management*, University of Warwick, 26–28 June.

Rosile, G. A., & Boardman, C. (2011). Antenarrative ethics of Native American Indian trading. In *Proceedings of the standing conference for management and organizational inquiry*, Philadelphia, PA.

Rosile, G. A., Pepion, D., Boje, D., & Gladstone, J. (2012). The ontology of diversity: Pedagogy for Native American ethics and philosophy. In *Research, pedagogy and other institutional practices: An interdisciplinary conference on diversity in higher education*, conference at New Mexico State University, Las Cruces, NM, March 9, 2012.

Rosile, G. A., Pepion, D., & Gladstone, J. (2012). Daniels principles of business ethics and tribal ethics: Using indigenous methods of storytelling to convey moral principles. In *January 2012 DFEI conference presentation*, Hotel Encanto, Las Cruces, NM.

Wilmoth, S. (2006). *Background for teachers: Some words on reciprocity*. Retrieved from http://www.his.state.mt.us/education/IEFALesson PlanTradeBarter.pdf (posted 2006; downloaded June 2010). Montana State Historic Preservation Office.

Indigenous Ways of Knowing and Quantum Science for Business Ethics

Donald D. Pepion

When I was learning ceremony from our holy people, I encountered an impasse in the process. Although I had been observing the rituals and liturgies of our spiritual traditions for many years, I had recently made the spiritual vow to be a member of the medicine bundle society. Knowing the protocol, I sought an individual consultation with my teachers, the bundle keepers commonly called medicine people.

After the smudging and prayer, the holy couple asked me what I needed. I explaining my perceived predicament, and since they knew my life history and story, they were able to readily respond. One of them stated, "We know you were not raised this way" and "maybe there are some things you didn't get as a child." "We know you go to that school over there with those other folks" was another comment.

Later, with some critical thinking, I was able to discern that I was using the Whiteman's logic and reasoning to make sense out of ceremonial learning. I also remembered that the childhood "Napi" stories, filled with metaphor and morals, were never translated or interpreted. In the Pikuni (Blackfeet) way of knowing the origin narratives include childhood stories. Napi was the first human who occupied the earth. He was partly divine as he could communicate with animate and inanimate beings of the world and the cosmos. Napi was sometimes nearly magical, possessing extraordinary powers. However, he possessed human qualities in that he was fallible, made mistakes, and sometimes did foolish things.

In other words, Napi is like us as human beings, we have great minds and abilities to do amazing feats. Yet, he was not perfect and like us as humans he sometimes made poor choices with disastrous effects. Napi could be comical as well as serious and caring. He was adventurous and willing to try new things.

In the Napi oral stories, the child has to critically think and make meaning of the story. Although, there are clearly consequences of Napi's behavior and actions, the storyteller usually does not "tell the moral of the story" so to speak, as with the European childhood fables. Thus, in the Pikuni (Blackfeet) way the individual child has to learn that life is about choices that many times have consequences. I believe this is the ultimate of freedom.

Individuals are free to make choices. We all know that if we tell a child not to touch a hot fire, they will probably experiment and feel the pain of potential burn. However, if we tell them a story about someone getting burned the chances are greater they will not try to experience the consequence.

When I returned to learning ceremony by experience and observation after talking to the elders, I determined not to use the Whiteman's logic and reasoning to make sense out of the process. I told myself, "I am a like a baby," I have to open my mind to all possibilities and not judge the experience from my over 20 years of so-called "education." At that point, my learning began with the Pikuni "way of knowing." I now know there is another way of finding "truth."

It is fairly well-known that Native American oral tradition is infused with storytelling. There has been some movement to equate quantum storytelling with indigenous ways of knowing (IWOK). One of the first questions scholars and others may ask about each of these subjects is "What is it?"

The theory and principles of quantum storytelling, especially with Dr. David Boje, has been rapidly emerging. Although his quantum storytelling is currently under the guise of the academic discipline of business, it has some multidisciplinary concepts. In turn, IWOK has been outside the realm of most academic disciplines but many scholars embrace the idea of it having holistic concepts and principles. Thus, we are on the cutting edge of exploring knowledge that may simultaneously have ancient roots but contain unchartered boundaries. Few critical scholars are willing to investigate knowledge that is outside the borders of academic disciplines. The risks are many but glimpses of futurist possibilities are intriguing.

Scholars will readily agree the terms epistemology and ontology are known concepts in Western knowledge. Since the Eurocentric age of reason has defined the world, anything outside of logic and reason is relegated to nihilism. Therefore, IWOK is labeled as primitive and nonsensical. If instrumentation and quantification cannot validate IWOK as reliable knowledge, than it is illogical nonsense to Western science.

Nonetheless, Western science has pilfered many aspects of IWOK as evidenced by pharmaceuticals, food-ways, cosmology, and more. Although most scholars and scientists will admit there is a vast unknown, they fear banishment and ridicule from the academy when exploring these kinds of knowledge. With the rise of Native scholars like Deloria, Wildcat, Cajete, Little Bear, Battiste, Henderson, and others, the doors are beginning to open to the profound philosophy and knowledge of indigenous people.

Native scholars are cautious about the "takers" and "travelers" who continue to *exploit* and *appropriate* Native knowledge as articulated by Maori author Linda Tuhiwai Smith. Ever since Justice Marshall in 1823 used the doctrine of discovery to claim ownership of American Indian lands, indigenous people know that the Euro-Americans will use their reason and logic in convoluted ways to justify the purloining of land and knowledge.

Both Deloria and Smith acknowledge the *discoverers* are adept at taking only those parts of indigenous knowledge that fit with their imperialistic viewpoints. The guarding of indigenous

UNIVERSITY OF WINCHESTER LIBRARY

intellectual property takes vigilance and acute attention by indigenous scholars on matters of research and study. The collaboration of quantum storytelling and indigenous knowledge can be a precarious journey. Native and academic scholars must be attuned to ethical boundaries and trust in the process of how cultures create truth.

Search for Wisdom

— Dr. Grace Ann Rosile

1. Pepion says the "IWOK is labeled as primitive and nonsensical."

   Why do you think this happens? Can you give an example?

2. Quantum science has similar findings about the nature of the world as those reached by IWOK. Can you give some examples of this? (Hint: Repeating patterns or fractiles are considered significant in both knowledge systems.)

3. Pepion notes that the Blackfeet way of raising children is to let them be free to make choices. Rather than telling a child a rule like "Don't touch the fire," Pepion recommends telling a story about someone who touched the fire and was badly burned. Do you think you could try Pepion's storytelling method with children? With young adults? With employees? Could you give an example that you tried, or might try, of a story used to convey a moral lesson to one of these audiences?

Grace Ann's Note

Many thanks to Dr. Don Pepion for his contribution to this volume, and his wise and insightful guidance throughout the Tribal Wisdom project!

In the next section, Dr. Lisa Grayshield discusses further aspects of IWOK. Dr. Grayshield is of the Washoe tribe, and is a behavioral scientist who has studied ways in which the Euro-Western science of counseling may be made more compatible with IWOK. Here, she discusses how IWOK requires a reframing of the relationship of business to society and to the environment.

The reframing of the people-profit-planet relationship can be seen as reflecting the second of the Eight Aspects of Tribal Wisdom, Gifting. Business needs to give back, to both society and to the environment, to balance what it takes from people and planet.

3

Indigenous Ways of Knowing and Business Sustainability

Lisa Grayshield

Wisdom of the Elders

Well-known indigenous scholar Deloria Jr. posed a question regarding the western scientific view of knowledge formation. He recorded the following answer of one tribal chief:

> Not bad, or untrue, but inadequate to explain among many other things how man is to find and know a road along which he wishes and chooses to make this said progress unless the Great Manitoo by his spirit guides the mind of man, keeping human beings just and generous and hospitable (p. 65).

In a conversation with an old Teton Sioux Indian, Deloria Jr. (1999) said of the Western scientific method:

> There is no difficulty in leading an old Teton Sioux Indian to understand the "scientific" attitude, and that the processes that give rise to phenomena may be more

and more known by man and be, to some extent, controlled by man and that in this way the forces of nature may become a mainspring of progress in the individual and in the human race. The idea of atoms and electrons is easy and pleasing to an old Indian and he grasps the idea of chemistry. Such things make ready contact with his previous observations and thinking ... . The world is constantly creating itself because everything is alive and making choices, which determine the future. (p. 63)

Deloria Jr. goes on to conclude from his research with Indigenous/Tribal elders that:

[t]here is a direction to the universe empirically exemplified in the physical growth cycles of childhood, youth and old age with the corresponding responsibility of every entity to enjoy life, fulfill itself, and increase in wisdom and spiritual development of personality. (p. 46)

This is true for all relationships according to Deloria Jr.'s research, including the relationships one develops with nature and spirit.

IWOK have served as a corner stone for addressing the challenges of global climate change and eco-sustainability. It is receiving increased attention in a variety of academic disciplines such as anthropology, sociology, psychology, engineering, and business. Chief Seattle stated this basic philosophic stance underlying an IWOK philosophy in his response to the US government's demand for ownership of the land in the 1850 treaty negotiations, "This we know, that all things are connected like the blood that unites us. We did not weave the web of life, we are merely a strand in it—whatever we do to the web, we do to ourselves" (Jeffers, 1991).

Preverbal Web of Existence — Indigenous knowledge is grounded deep within every culture on the planet. It begins with the innate understanding that all things are alive and important in the preverbal web of existence. Chief Seattle's words were more than simply a statement of environment awareness to the impending foreign reign. Rather they were a plea to respect the earth as the Mother of all beings including the plant nations, the four leggeds, the ones that fly, swim, and crawl upon the earth. Chief Seattle's words have been memorialized in children's books and journal articles and on environmental posters for centuries, but have had little impact in a world of gross national product (GNP).

Contradictory Paradigms? — There are no "known" forms of knowledge in the Indigenous conception of the universe for which to apply evidence-based practices to achieve material gain. Indigenous knowledge applied to business ethics would render the pursuits of material gain contradictory in its most genuine expression. IWOK encompasses a way to think about the world that includes respect for all beings on the planet, including the life of the non-human world.

A business paradigm that professes IWOK is cognizant of the interdependence and interconnectedness of all life on the planet. IWOK operates to ensure that our grandchildren's grandchildren will experience the beauty and abundance of Mother Earth. The purpose for this chapter is to provide the foundational concepts of IWOK that informs a paradigm that is effectively indigenous.

IWOK Defined — IWOK has been defined as a multidimensional body of lived experiences that informs and sustains people who make their homes in a local area. It always takes into account the current socio-political colonial power dimensions of the Western world (Denzin, Lincoln, & Tuhiwai Smith, 2008).

Three Features — The literature identifies three central features within Indigenous knowledge that have both political and curricular implications. One feature is that Indigenous/Tribal cultures related harmoniously to their environments. A second feature is that these cultures experienced colonization. A third feature is that these cultures provided an alternative perspective on human experience that differed from Western empirical science (p. 144).

The first feature of this definition of IWOK refers to numerous forms of knowledge construction by Indigenous/Tribal groups that have allowed them to maintain their existence in a specific locale over time. This includes the combined paradigms of their epistemologies, ontologies, and cosmologies that construct ways of being and experiencing in relationship to their physical surroundings (Kincheloe & Steinberg, as cited in Denzin et al., 2008).

The three central features (relating harmoniously to one's environment; the experience of colonization; an alternative perspective on human experience that is different from Western empirical science) provide a practical frame for application of a venture that intends to produce a positive impact in service of sustainability of the natural environment as well as in consideration for its abundant beauty for generations to come.

Relating Harmoniously to One's Environment

The Maya — One of the most profound literary accounts of IWOK that has proven practical in many different aspects of today's world is represented by the Mayan calendar. A "stone age people" called the Maya were described by Arguelles (1987). Arguelles saw these people as scientists whose observations of the known universe extended beyond the material cognitive constructs of modern science. These observations included a deeper and more meaningful understanding that is based on harmonic resonance. This resonance is like an "invisible galactic life thread" that links people, the planet, the sun, and the center of the Galaxy.

Harmonic Resonance — According to Arguelles (1987), as a society whose ways of knowing are based on harmonic resonance, the Maya society recognizes the influence of numerous constructs of the natural environment. This society recognized not only the senses, but also levels and frequencies of synchronized intelligence from altered states of consciousness. They recognized a range from the smallest particle of matter to the vastness of the universe itself.

Balance — From Arguelles' description of the Mayan ways of knowing, business ventures might stand to gain tremendous advances by recognizing factors associated with harmonic resonance. Business ventures might adopt the "goal" of studying IWOK to assist with the processes of reaching a balanced state of existence with the planet. This balance would recognize the effect of the resonance of GNP on the relationships that we establish with each other and with the environment.

An Alternative Paradigm — IWOK offers the world an alternative to the more familiar Western scientific paradigm of GNP in which we currently operate. With an IWOK worldview, numerous business ventures would be rendered inoperable, and inherently unintelligent. A business paradigm which incorporated IWOK would naturally consider the impact that its business ventures are having on the natural environment. It would consider the thousands of years of lived experience where sustainability, balance, and harmony in a community is intricately interwoven with the natural environment.

Social Uprising — There is currently an uprising against genetically modified organisms in food production (GMO). Such GMOs are an example of the inherent disregard of context, both socially and environmentally, of business ventures whose sole purpose is to raise its profit margin. This disregard and dismissal of any questioning of the GNP business paradigm has resulted in the current profound and significant social uprising.

Food Production — One example of the disregard for the natural state of the environment is the company Monsanto, originally a producer of pesticides and industrial chemicals and more recently is known as the largest seed company in the world. A short tour on Ted talks and YouTube of Monsanto's impact on US soldiers, US farmers, their crops, the land and other people and nations around the world reveals a worldwide epidemic. Lessons learned from the ill effect of the production and ingestion of chemical pesticides and GMO foods have much to offer in our efforts to rethink business ventures that include food production.

In sum, the culmination of wisdom teachings from ancient traditions is central to IWOK. One need not look too far to conceive the shift in paradigm praxis that must take place in promoting harmonious relationships with all beings on the planet, including the plant nations, the water, and the earth in general. The wisdom of IWOK becomes readily apparent when one spends sometime in the vibration of nature, reflecting on the impact that one's life has had, and what one's perceived life purpose has been.

Search for Wisdom

— Dr. Grace Ann Rosile

1. Could you write, or find on the Internet, a business vision statement that addresses the preservation and respect for ancient wisdom?

2. Could you write, or find on the Internet, a business mission/vision statement that considers promotion of balance and of harmony with the natural environment? (Hints: Patagonia, Buffalo Exchange, Seventh Generation)

3. Would you be interested in understanding the critical concepts of interconnection and interdependence as presented in the Medicine Wheel, also referred to as the Wheel of Life?

4. Can you find some examples of business efforts which are moving in the direction of a Medicine Wheel or IWOK way of operating? You might consider the topic of Corporate Social Responsibility (CSR), the Triple Bottom Line (people, product, planet), or others.

5. What evidence do you see (if any) that such efforts to create balance and harmony, both socially and environmentally, are increasing? Is there more you would like to see?

> **Grace Ann's Note**
>
> Many thanks to Dr. Lisa Grayshield for her contribution to this volume! She assists us in our desire to see the world through each other's eyes, in ways that may benefit all.
>
> In the next chapter, Dr. Gregory Cajete explains how indigenous understanding of the interdependence of all life provides a basis for indigenous ethical values and practices. This respect for our interdependent relationships applies to current-day businesses as well as to the environment. An ecology of economics is created in traditions which share wealth, such as the potlatch.
>
> These concepts of reciprocal behavior, sharing wealth, and ecology, all are life-enhancing ways to foster the sustainability of our business world. Sharing wealth contributes to the third Aspect of Tribal Wisdom, Egalitarianism. Mutual reciprocal behavior incorporates the second Aspect of Tribal Wisdom, Gifting.

References

Arguelles, J. (1987). *The Mayan factor: Path beyond technology.* Santa Fe, NM: Bear & Company Publishing.

Deloria, V., Jr. (1999). *Spirit and reason.* Golden, CO: Fulcrum Publishing.

Denzin, N. K., Lincoln, Y. S., & Tuhiwai Smith, L. (2008). *Handbook of critical and Indigenous methodologies.* Los Angeles, CA: Sage.

Jeffers, S. (1991). *Brother eagle, sister sky: A message from Chief Seattle.* New York, NY: Dial Books.

Indigenous Science for Business Ethics and the Environment

4

Gregory Cajete with cases by Grace Ann Rosile

I am Gregory Cajete, from Santa Clara Pueblo, "one of the people." I was a field biologist, with a second major in sociology at New Mexico Highlands University. I intended to go on in biology, but then I was offered a position at a post-secondary school. I was asked to be a high school biology/science teacher, and I was given the task to integrate science and art.

This job allowed me to explore creative solutions, ways to communicate science to students interested in the arts. I began to diagnose the educational process. I had to look at basic assumptions, and ask myself what is education. This led me to a very deep examination of indigenous epistemologies, and the evolution of native communities, in the process of creating this curriculum.

Business and Indigenous Science — What does this have to do with business? It has everything to do with business. Business is one of those human cultural enterprises which are very steeped in the values and ethics and foundations, of a community, of a culture, of a tradition, and of a way of living in the world. So business has everything to do with indigenous science, and vice versa.

Complementary World Views — There are many ways that business and tribal culture can complement each other. The indigenous world view is very different. But we need to remember that there was a time when that world view was the view of all human cultures. This indigenous world view involved a deep and intimate relationship with the natural world and with each other. And out of that comes the process, as we would say, of "doing business."

Today the indigenous world view and the western world view seem worlds apart. That was especially apparent when I began to study what was going on with the art students at the Santa Fe Institute with regard to their resistance to science. This resistance was there because at the very deepest levels there was resistance to the whole world view that gave rise to that western type of science. And likewise, the resistance of western science and western business to indigenous ideas and perspectives is also a cultural kind of thing. These resistances are based on the differences in evolutions and histories and ways of thinking and ways of being in the world.

Business in Relationship to the Natural World — We have to begin to find ways to view business in different kinds of ways. We seek ways that are more life-sustaining, ways that in a sense, allow us to begin to develop a better kind of relationship with the natural world. The natural world is the source and resource for all forms of business.

Mutual Reciprocal Behavior — I draw the idea of "mutual reciprocal behavior" from biological sciences. There are visible ways in which there is a mutual reciprocal behavioral process. There is a give and take, with regard to the transactions which human beings have with the natural world.

This reciprocity is an ethical concept. It's give, but also receive, and receive and also give, and doing it in a process that enhances both sides of the equation. That "mutual reciprocal behavior" is very much an ethical principle. It deals with relationship. It deals with building and honoring relationships, so that idea of relationality comes through. It is a very direct and very powerful lens that needs to be reflected in today's business world.

Business and Community — Another area of concern is community, in the sense that businesses are parts of community, they rely on community for their existence. The process of giving back to community in some very direct and tangible ways is a part, not only of the business ethic, but also as a part of the way you do business, and why you do business. All these considerations become an integral part of business.

These relationship-oriented ethical considerations for business include honesty, trustworthiness, and respect for the clients that you have in your business. You need an understanding that you're in business because of them, because of them buying your product or buying your service.

Potlatch — A classic example that is often given with regard to mutual reciprocal behavior would be the potlatch. Many tribes in the northwest practiced, and continue to practice today, the potlatch. The goal of the potlatch is not to accumulate wealth. The goal is to be able to give as much wealth away as possible, knowing and understanding that somewhere in this continuum of mutual reciprocal behavior that you would then be given back much of what you have given away. It may be that you would be given back in some new forms.

Share Wealth — That idea of mutual reciprocal behavior has been internalized in the traditional forms of the northwest Indian "Potlatch" as a social institution. It was society's way to redistribute wealth, to accumulate status. Yet at the same time, this process insured that the community, the society as a whole, benefitted from the enterprise and the wealth, the trading and the bartering, the business, if you will. Everyone would have at least a share of the good fortune.

Deep Ethics — Ethics do matter in business, and deep ethics, and deep ethical values, in many ways, is what we need today. We are very good in terms of business as a system, as operations. We know the details of how transactions should be done, and the kinds of criteria for management. But what is missing many times is that ethical dimension, that reason or meaning or purpose for business, and that has to come back, very directly, in a very extensive way, in today's business world.

Web of Interaction — I would simply say that there is value in understanding that business is a part of a web, is part of a complex adaptive system as we would call it in the biological sciences. There are multiple kinds of interactions that simultaneously affect one's behavior, and one's work, and one's way of doing business. You have to be aware of those interactions and their impacts in terms of the total ecology of what is happening with an industry, a community, or an economic system.

Ecology of Economics — I think that we have a sense of the complexity of economic systems today, but we don't have a sense of its complex ecology. And what's missing from that complex ecology is the purpose for doing business. And so, in terms of business, I would say that business must now become a part of the human ecology, for many reasons. Ultimately, business must become a part of the human ecology to avoid its own demise. We're part of nature, we're not separate from it. The same principles that operate in the ecologies of animal communities, of plant communities, also operate in human communities, but in, of course, human ways.

Privileging Relationship — We have this idea of privileging the relationship. There is an ethic, a value, of privileging these concepts that deal with respect, and privileging this view of understanding what you do within a context of a greater whole. And I think also, understanding that doing business is very, very predicated on relationship. But that relationship includes not only relationship to other people, or to a community, but also relationship to other sources and resources that you use to create your business.

Ecological Foundation of Business — And so, there is that human-nature connection that has to be re-established with regard to the practice of business. That is the ecological foundation of business. I think that that's a lesson that has endured for many decades now. We are learning that ignoring that ecological foundation of business is going to cost us dearly. There is no doubt in my mind that we are going to have to change dramatically, in the way that we work with each other, in the way that we treat each other, interact with each other, if we are going to truthfully, truthfully survive into the next decades.

The understandings and world views of indigenous people were based, in a sense, on long-term survivability with the environments. This understanding has to now become part of that formula that we use to do business and to interact with the natural world. This indigenous understanding of interdependency has to become part of our re-formation of human society. In the next 100 years of doing business, we will begin to move toward that place-based kind of understanding of relationship. We will in a sense bring ecology back to business, in a way that is life-enhancing.

CASE VIGNETTE

"The Business of Culture at Acoma Pueblo"
— *Dr. Grace Ann Rosile*

If you go online and search for Acoma Pueblo Case Study, or "The Business of Culture at Acoma Pueblo: Case Study and Teaching Notes" you will find the story of how this Pueblo tribe went from a small souvenir stand to a thriving tourist business complete with a Cultural Center with restaurant, guided tours with bus transportation to the entrance of the ancient pueblo, films, displays, museum-quality art and artifacts, and more. The information in this vignette is taken from that on-line case example. To see the full case, try this link:

http://www.unm.edu/~hmuller/The%20Business%20of%20Culture%20at%20Acoma%20Pueblo.htm

A woman, Mary Tenorio, had brought structure, order, and sound bookkeeping practices to the old souvenir stand of earlier days. She was a guiding force behind the growth and development of Acoma's cultural tourism. However, she encountered many difficulties along the way.

Hers was a matriarchal society. In this particular society, this meant the women owned the houses, and passed them down to their youngest daughters. The men sat on the Tribal Council, which did not allow women members. Only the Tribal Council had authority to make business decisions for the tribe. Mary Tenorio could not be a member of the Council. How could she promote the business changes she knew were needed to develop the tribe's "Business of Culture?"

If you are like me and most business school graduates, your first thought likely would be "Change the system." If the system interferes with making a profit, then the system is wrong. Change the system. After all, companies change policies every day of the week to maintain profits.

The question was not so simple for Mary. If she tried to change this centuries-old tradition, she would be violating some of the very tribal norms that the desired Cultural Center was designed to preserve.

QUESTION 1. What would you have advised Mary Tenorio to do?

Consider: In the fall of 2007, a group of us attended a conference at Acoma's modern new Sky City Casino Hotel. We were in a typical carpeted hotel conference room the afternoon of our presentation with 15–20 people in attendance. We were excited about sharing our research with this group, the Federation of Indigenous Business and Entrepreneurship. One of our best and brightest graduate students stood up. He was enthusiastic, poised, and professional in his dark business suit. He began our role-play exercise by making his "elevator pitch" (very focused, 1–2 minute business proposal) to our hypothetical "tribal council" (the audience members). We did not expect what happened next.

Barely a sentence into his presentation, an angry woman stood up and said "What is wrong with you young man? Where are your manners?" Our student stopped cold, a confused look on his face. She proceeded to berate him for not addressing the hypothetical "tribal council" in proper fashion, and for not introducing himself properly. Chastened, he began again, identifying his tribal lineage, and using respectful words to address the council.

Maybe Mary Tenorio went through something like this. Or maybe she avoided such embarrassment because, as you can read in the extensive online case about Acoma, Mary Tenorio consulted her father on how to work with and through the Tribal Council. By working together respectfully to innovate while also honoring tradition, Mary and the tribe achieved the success they enjoy today.

QUESTION 2. After becoming successful with a thriving cultural tourist business, Acoma was faced with another dilemma. Should they remain closed, as had been their practice, during sacred feast days and ceremonies? Or should they open these events to tourists?

What would you recommend: closed or open? And why?

Grace Ann's Note

Many thanks to Dr. Gregory Cajete for his contribution to this volume! He has reminded us of the importance of Tribal Wisdom Aspect #1, Relationship, as the foundation of all tribal values. We will hear Dr. Cajete's voice again in later sections, regarding storytelling as well as sustainability. Sustainability is a key factor in relationships, as indigenous relationships are grounded in the core concept of humans in relation to the natural world and our Mother Earth.

Balancing respectful relationships with business considerations was the theme of the short case vignette presented above. In the summarization of the online case example "The Business of Culture at Acoma Pueblo" we see how Mary Tenorio put into practice the value of relationships and respect before profit. She worked within her tribal governance structures to promote economic improvements.

In the next chapter, I offer an overview of approaches to business ethics. I trace trends towards group-oriented, relationship-focused ethics which are directions already compatible with values of American Indian tribal cultures.

5

Business Ethics Overview and Current Trends

Grace Ann Rosile with cases by Mabel Sanchez

This chapter places indigenous ethics in its relationships with the recent Euro-Western literature on business ethics. I offer several different categories of approaches which have emerged from philosophers over the years. These approaches are summarized in Table 5.1: Business Ethics Overview and Comparison of Approaches. This chapter concludes with a four-quadrant model of businesses (Rosile, 2014) as either Elders, Masters, Migrators, or Traders, depending on whether they offer a product or service, and whether they operate predominantly in their home culture or across cultural borders.

Rules-Based — First in our Business Ethics Overview table is the deontological or "follow the rules" approach to ethics, based on the work of Kant (1785/2002) and others. Kant says we have certain rules and we are supposed to follow them. Sometimes people say "just do what is right." But then the question becomes, how do you know what is right? And what if someone else thinks something different is right? And what if doing what is right might result in harm to someone? So sometimes there is confusion. How do we weigh factors in complex situations where the right thing to do is not clear?

The rules-based approach might be seen in the ways in which tribal cultures use ceremony and rituals to restore balance and harmony. An example might be the rituals followed for a hunt, making peace with the spirit of the animal. There are prayers at the outset of an undertaking, to bring success. In Chapter 11, Dr. Cal Boardman discusses how trust was built among tribal traders by following rules and social norms for trading practices. Those practices included full and voluntary disclosure of any problems involved with a trade agreement. Such socially agreed-upon rules facilitated trading relationships.

Virtue — Another long-standing tradition in ethics is "virtue" ethics, rooted in Aristotle's (350 BC/1954) philosophy. Virtue ethics says that people should do what a virtuous person would do. A kind person, a person possessing the virtue of kindness, would do a kind act. You might say "By their fruits you will know them." So this approach values a virtuous person doing virtuous deeds.

The problem is what happens when you have a clash in virtuous behaviors: Do you tell someone a lie to be kind, or do you tell them a truth which would be hurtful? There can be clashes between which virtues apply in a situation.

In terms of Tribal Wisdom, Aspect #2, Gifting, is an example of a virtue in tribal cultures. Aspect #4, Non-Acquisitiveness, or not taking more than one needs, reflects the other side of the coin. Translated into daily behaviors, practicing these virtues means that in many indigenous cultures, the person who gives is respected more than the person who acquires more than they need. There is further discussion of both rules and virtues in terms of tribal ethical teachings in Chapter 10 of this book (Verbos, Kennedy, & Claw, 2016).

Utilitarian/Consequential — The consequential or utilitarian approach to ethics is based on the work of Bentham (1987) and Mill (1861/1987), among others. This approach says a person should work towards the greatest good for the greatest number of people. This is a more social-oriented view. It is often accepted that you may have to sacrifice the few to save the many. The focus here is on what is the outcome of a person's act? Morality is judged not based on the act itself, but rather on the outcome of the act, and who is affected. This is a very rational kind of calculation of ethical-ness. A criticism of this approach is can people actually know and calculate the outcomes of alternative courses of action? And if they can, do people actually stop and make such calculations in real life? Further, what happens when a particular group of people's good is always sacrificed to the benefit of another particular group? Might some small groups be systematically disadvantaged?

A utilitarian type of reasoning supports Tribal Wisdom Aspect #4, Non-Acquisitiveness, because it is presumed that if one takes (acquires) more than one needs to live, this might prevent another from having what they need to live. This also relates to Aspect #5, Usefulness. If we are not using something, we are potentially hoarding a resource others might need. We ought to let it go to someone who would use that resource.

Equity — The "equity" approach to ethics is based on concepts of justice and rights (Rawls, 1971/1999 among others). This again is a social and relational view of ethics. It says we need fairness. We all seem to have an innate sense of what is fair. We have probably all heard little toddlers cry "No fair!" when another child grabs their toy. This perspective is another social view of ethics, a view which looks at interpersonal behaviors, not just at an individual who may be virtuous or not. How am I treating others? Is this treatment fair and equitable? One criticism of the group/social view of fairness is that it does not consider ways to resolve previous unfairness such as slavery, genocide, and other historical examples of widespread unfair treatment.

Non-Acquisitiveness, Tribal Wisdom Aspect #8, might also be considered part of an equity-based approach to ethics. Non-Acquisitiveness presumes that each is entitled to what they need, but not to more than that. Taking more than one needs is considered greed, because it could mean taking someone else's fair share of goods.

Answerability — Another very recent approach to ethics is based on the work of Bakhtin (1990, 1993), called "Answerability."

This is perhaps the most proactive approach to ethics. This approach says that because each of our lives is unique and different, that we are faced with unique opportunities, opportunities that no one else has.

Answerability says you are answerable, you are responsible, for acting in that moment of your life, in a way that only you can act. You have a responsibility to have an impact that only you can have, because nobody else can do what you can do in that moment. The other side of this is the implication of not acting. If we take no action, we are complicit in permitting, condoning, allowing, or even perhaps promoting the circumstances to which we have failed to respond.

Answerability can be seen in Tribal Wisdom Aspect #8, Disclosure. Disclosure means full and voluntary telling of potential problems in a business transaction. It means taking initiative and volunteering information even before one is asked.

Obligation to Act — Thus according to answerability, we have an ethical obligation to take initiative, to be proactive. This may involve contradicting social norms or what others are doing. Nelson Mandela contradicted norms of behavior to the extent that he was imprisoned for much of his life. Reverend Bob and his wife Jeannie Graetz (personal communication), a white couple with three children, moved to Alabama from Ohio in the 1960s when no one else wanted to go to serve that ministry. They stood with Dr. Martin Luther King in the civil rights protests of that era. They persisted, despite their house being bombed twice.

Proactive, not Complicit — If we are not proactive in taking action to support our ethical values, then we run the risk of being complicit. Complicit means that through inaction, we condone or permit actions that violate our ethical standards. Sherron Watkins (personal communication), when she saw the potentially illegal and (to her) unethical actions of Enron, stepped forward to bring these behaviors to light. When then-CEO Ken Lay ignored her seven-page memo outlining her concerns, she ultimately testified in court regarding what she saw, leading to convictions of top executives.

In less-dramatic circumstances than Watkins, Mandela, or the Graetz', consider an everyday business situation. A joke based on a racial slur gets lots of laughs. The person who objects to the joke is acting in an answerable fashion. Most philosophers agree that the most advanced stage of moral development is when someone acts based on a higher moral principle even when that involves acting in opposition to group norms or even in opposition to civil laws. This view puts individual action within a social context, taking into account the social norms and the impact of one's actions on others.

Ethics of Care — The ethics of care is another perspective, rooted in observing parents, mothers, caregivers of children, and of the elderly, and in general those who give care to valued members of our society (Gilligan, 1982; Held, 2006; among others). This view recognizes the importance of such care-giving in all its many forms, for the maintenance of important social relationships such as family ties. What kind of society would we be if we did not honor and care for our elders and our children?

The ethics of care says whatever contributes to caring human relationships is ethical. Included in this view of ethics is not only the action, but also the intention, such as the intention to be loving and caring. Being caring includes the intention and the feeling underlying the act of being caring. We can't fake being caring. You might summarize this as "Do Unto Others" or as "All You Need is Love." Critics see this social/relational view as potentially susceptible to over-emotionality and favoritism.

The "Ethics of Care" has the same basic foundation in relationships which is the core of Tribal Wisdom. We see many overlaps and compatibilities in these two perspectives.

Pragmatism — Another ethical approach is the more recent perspective called pragmatism (Dewey, 1920, 1938, and others). Pragmatism is also more inclusive of the other perspectives. Pragmatism is relational and socially oriented, because it invokes the quantum-physics-oriented implications for the connectedness (entanglement) of all life. Pragmatists consider how "reality" and present time is greatly affected by past experience as well as by anticipations of the future. Pragmatists avoid specific statements of right and wrong. Instead, they rely on a person's connectedness (or "attunement") to guide each individual to know what is right and what is wrong.

Some pragmatists say you do not just pick the approach you like when facing an ethical dilemma. You have an obligation to seek wisdom and guidance on how to make difficult ethical choices. Pragmatists acknowledge principles and sets of virtues, but they avoid hard-and-fast rules. Similarly, Tribal Wisdom's approach avoids hard-and-fast rules in favor of principles, and in favor of individuals seeking their own understanding of what is right, along with consultation with elders and spirit guides.

Comparison to Indigenous Philosophies — Pragmatism's aspects of connectedness and the blurring of lines between past-present-future times make pragmatism very compatible with indigenous philosophy. Similarly, the ethics of care incorporates the tribal tradition of the primary importance of relationships. However, the ethics of care approach does not typically include nature. Indigenous relationships include relations with the earth and the natural environment, which are also considered to be alive and of equal or superior status compared to humans.

Overlap — We find that in each of these perspectives of ethics presented in Table 5.1, there is some area of overlap with indigenous values at a broad level. We are not looking at specific teachings like the Seven Grandfather Teachings. Instead, we are looking at a more general level. When we talk to people from indigenous tribes, and see what indigenous scholars have written, what principles have emerged as endorsed by many? Especially in the business context, where people have exchanges with others, what are the guiding principles for making that exchange not only ethical, but economically successful, viable, and sustainable?

When viewed as a whole, Table 5.1 demonstrates a trend away from an individual view of ethics towards a more collective perspective in approaches to ethics. At the top the focus is on the individual's actions in the categories of Deontological and Virtue. Consequential and Rights approaches consider the individual in relation to others. Ethics of care endorses the value of caring actions as most important to holding together the fabric of society, so moral rightness is based on the impact of an action on important social relationships. Pragmatism suggests that humans are all connected or "entangled," so morality may be determined either by an individual-focused model like deontology or virtue ethics, or by a socially focused model like consequential or rights approaches to ethics. Indigenous ethics takes the pragmatic approach a step farther, by including in the web of relationships the plants and animals and all of the natural world.

The trend in business ethics literature overall is towards a more relationship-oriented and societal level view of ethics. These trends may be new for today's corporate world, but they have always featured prominently in the indigenous world, as the bedrock of indigenous values and ethics. In sum, we see increasing relevance of indigenous traditions, values, and practices to the current trends in business ethics, as we discuss in next paragraphs.

Shrinking World and the Global Village — Globalization, the role of the Internet, and the ability to have communications, relationships, and transactions with people around the planet, contribute to our "shrinking world." This shrinking world trend makes us more than ever aware of the quality of our relationships with our neighbors around the globe. The corporate environment is increasingly becoming a global village. Already, we see glimmers of most of these practices rooted in indigenous traditions showing up in contemporary businesses.

Giving — For an example of the presence of tribal practices already appearing in American businesses, we consider one of the Eight Aspects of Tribal Wisdom: Giving (or "gifting") rather than getting. Giving to others is viewed as a more desirable activity than getting material benefits for the self. In businesses today, we see a version of this in the increasing examples of businesses which offer free samples, free trial periods of use, free gifts with purchases, free Google accounts, etc.

Carry-over — These tribal wisdoms presented here will offer fresh insights into how business relationships may more fully reflect the caring attitudes and values which we desire in our larger societies. At the same time, it is equally important that tribal peoples see that their traditional values regarding the importance of such things as relationships, respect, giving, non-acquisitive non-greediness, trust, usefulness, and barter, may be carried into successful business transactions in the non-tribal business world.

Example — Book contributor Dr. Dan Stewart notes that when he practices indigenous-style trust by voluntarily disclosing potentially damaging information in business transactions with non-tribal organizations, this is well-received. His non-tribal business partners appreciate his honesty and see him as more trustworthy. This is in contrast to the (thankfully now largely outmoded) older historical practices of "Buyer Beware!" Most of today's businesses recognize the value of honesty and integrity and building trusting relationships.

It is our hope that tribal organizations will see new ways in which their traditions and practices can be not only accepted, but also viewed as important and even essential in non-tribal businesses. Tribal traditions can contribute to both economic success and as well as ethical and socially responsible conduct of business. Equally, businesses can find fresh ideas, inspiration for new practices, and greater awareness of already-successful tribal-values-oriented strategies in these pages.

The above discussion has addressed how different theoretical approaches to ethics focus attention on different aspects of moral behavior. Moving from the above overview of perspectives on business ethics, next is consideration of how different cross-cultural business contexts can give rise to different patterns of relevant ethical issues.

Table 5.1: Business Ethics Comparison of Approaches.

Ethical Approach	Simple Definition	Key Assumptions	Issues/Dilemmas	Morality Measured by
Rules-Based	Follow the rules	There are universal rules which always apply	Doing the "right" thing may result in harmful acts	Consistency (Truth, even if it hurts.)
Virtue	Act according to what a virtuous person would do	The person will recognize what is Good	Situations like euthanasia, where cruelty may be kindness	Intention (What would Jesus do?)
Consequential/ Utilitarian	Greatest Good for Greatest Number	The end justifies the means	Who benefits? At whose expense?	Outcome
Answerability	Be ethically proactive	A person is obliged to act if they see unethical behavior	Distinguishing between social responsibility and interfering with another's rights	Taking initiative and being proactive in doing what is right
Equity	Fairness within the social group	Looks beyond the individual	Life may not be fair; difficult to measure equity	Fair social distribution

Table 5.1: (Continued)

Ethical Approach	Simple Definition	Key Assumptions	Issues/Dilemmas	Morality Measured by
Ethics of Care	Do Unto Others	Caring interpersonal relationships are the goal of society	Emotionalism, Favoritism	Effect on interpersonal relationships
Indigenous	Live in balance and harmony	Includes the natural world	Appears to neglect individuals	Quality of all relationships, including the natural world
Pragmatism	In-the-moment connectedness	Considers the fluid nature of reality	Right and wrong depends on the context	Appropriateness to situation

Source: Adapted from Claw, Verbos, and Rosile (2017, forthcoming).

Four (4) Ethical Contexts for Businesses

Cultural Differences in Ethics — Businesses operating in different cultural contexts may face different ethical issues. Is a payment a bonus, a bribe, a kickback, or just a gift? What is acceptable and even required in one culture may be considered unethical, rude, or even illegal in another. We offer a framework of four (4) ethical contexts. The contexts allow us to identify the most likely ethical issues for that business, and the typical dangers and challenges arising in that cultural context.

We begin first with a distinction between businesses which operate primarily within their home culture (Internal) versus those that operate outside of their home culture (External). The second category is whether the business offers a service or business process, or instead is product or content-oriented. Table 5.2 suggests categories for a range of businesses based on these two dimensions of internal or external, and service/process or product/content.

"Elders" — First we consider the business that operates primarily within its home culture, and offers a service or business process. We call the story that this business tells, or the story by which it identifies itself, as the Elders Story. The Elders safeguard traditions, take the wisdom of historical leaders, and pass it on to future generations.

As an example of an Elders business story, we suggest the Blue Stone Consulting Group. They explicitly state, on their web site, that they want to help businesses create successful strategies while promoting tribal values in the current business environment.

The Navajo Nation Peacemakers also fall into the Elders category. They use the traditional Navajo peacemaking process to resolve disputes, and are a recognized alternative to our western judicial system. Our judicial system has been using the Peacemakers more and more, not to determine who is right and who is wrong. Instead, they are focused on healing relationships and returning the community to peacefulness, with harmony and balance being restored to conflicting parties.

Table 5.2: A Storytelling Model for Cross-Paradigm Business Ethics.

	Product is Service or Process	Product is Product or Content
Market is INTERNAL	**ELDERS Story** Service is expertise in processes, especially tribal traditions, while engaging in business **Examples** Blue Stone Consulting Group NOVA IT Security Navajo Nation Peacemakers **Danger:** tribal values being eroded or overcome by the dominant profit-first culture, leading to loss of market	**MASTERS Story** Product is a cultural artifact, Offered primarily to those within the culture, or those seeking "authentic" **Examples** Master Drum Makers (Yolanda) Potters, Weavers, Basket makers, Silversmiths, Dancers, Musicians, other arts/crafts **Danger:** devaluing the "authentic" in favor of the less expensive; changing cultural norms such that this "art" is no longer as highly valued
Market is EXTERNAL	**MIGRATORS Story** Service incorporates traditional tribal values while selling to the non-native market. **Examples** DarDan Enterprises (Sustainability) Restaurant (service values) **Danger:** value orientation reduces ability to be competitive and profitable	**TRADERS Story** Product is an artifact or by-product of the native world which is sold to the non-native market. **Examples** Casinos like Laguna Dev. Corp. Cigarette Distributors External Sales of "Authentic" Tribal Arts, Crafts, and Spiritual Practices and Events **Danger:** Commodification of spirituality and art, "selling out" of values in favor of profits

Source: Table from Rosile (2014), IACCM Conference Proceedings.

At the end of Part I of this volume, Mabel Sanchez provides a case example of NOVA Corporation. NOVA traces their information technology and security mission back to the Navajo Code Talkers. The Code Talkers used their Navajo language skills to put secret World War II information in the Navajo language, which the other side was unable to decode as they had with other encodings. Code Talkers are widely credited with shortening the war. In sum, Elders take traditional values and skills and carry them forward to resolve issues in business and society today.

"Masters" — If the business is focused on a product or content which is offered within the home culture, then we call the story that this kind of business tells, a Masters Story. The Master drum makers know the traditional ways of making a drum, the proper kind of drum, the proper spiritual blessing, whatever is involved. Potters, weavers, artists, musicians, all of them are masters of a traditional skill. In the marketplace, the danger that we see is what happens when mass production makes the same drum cheaper? Is it just as good, or isn't it? It is a controversial topic. Currently we see more and more businesses marketing themselves on the basis of "authentic" practices and "approved" master practitioners, who hold to the traditional ways of producing and conveying goods and services within that culture. Those are the Masters.

The danger here is the question of what we define as authentic. The same debate occurs even in leadership, what is the authentic leader, the authentic self? What is the difference between a generic drug and the name brand drug? It is that kind of argument. But there is a niche, and perhaps a growing niche, for organizations that capitalize on their traditionally recognized mastery.

"Migrators" — Some organizations operate externally to their home environment, whether globally or tribally. Those external businesses that offer a service or process to the outside world we call "Migrators." They are taking something of value from their home culture, and seeing that this can also be of value in another context, external to that business' home culture.

An example of a Migrator business appears in Gladstone (2012). He tells of an American Indian restauranteur whose business was off the reservation. This business owner talked of the giving of his best. For him, he was not just providing food for a reasonable price. Going beyond what was due or what was just good enough, he was offering the best that he had, as a form of gift.

Gift-giving, and the expectation that what is given is one's very best, is a tribal value that this restaurant owner exported or "migrated" into the non-indigenous culture. As a matter of pride and identity, success was earned by offering the best. With Migrators, the integrity and the values that come from within the culture are migrated outside that culture. The risk here is similar to that with Masters, with the question of whether the outside world will recognize and value that kind of gift, that skill or quality of service or product.

"Traders" — Finally, the businesses that operate external to their home environment, and offer a product or a content, are called "Traders." They take their home products or knowledge, and trade with the outside world. For example, Navajo rugs are very valuable in the external marketplace. American Indian silver jewelry enjoys successful trade with the non-indigenous world.

Casinos are another example of a successful tribal business marketed to primarily non-indigenous customers. However, despite their profitability, there is some controversy over whether casinos are good or bad for Indian country. Some tribal people may say they do not think it is good for tribal members to work in such an environment, where drinking and gambling may attract an already-at-risk population.

On the other side of the controversy, many see the opportunity to take the profits from casinos, which are made possible by the different legal status of reservation businesses, and funnel those profits into the development of businesses more in harmony with perceived indigenous values. Similarly, an indigenous distributor of cigarettes may use the distribution channels developed in this profitable market niche to then offer other, less controversial products, via the same channels of distribution.

There have been abuses by some "Trader" businesses where people purport to offer, for example, "authentic" native spiritual experiences such as sweat lodges (see Gladstone & Claw, 2015). These "authentic" experiences are being sold to the non-indigenous world. Gladstone and Claw report a very dramatic example of dangers inherent in such practices. In one case, three people died in a sweat-lodge experience which had been marketed to non-indigenous customers. The danger is with contamination from the outside world, with selling anything that will bring in dollars without regard to authenticity or respect for sacred cultural traditions. On the other hand, we see "Trader" businesses that take steps to protect themselves, and use their profits to support tribal values and practices.

In sum, we find a helpful distinction in considering a business' home culture, and how business may be conducted within and outside of that culture. We see that different types of ethical issues are more relevant in each of the four (4) different categories of Elders, Masters, Migrators, and Traders.

The 4-quadrant model highlights differences in the ethical issues for businesses operating in different contexts, especially when they operate outside of their home culture. One of the most important ethical issues in such a cross-cultural context is power. In order for trading relationships to be ethical at their core, at their most basic level, these trading relationships tend to be more ethical when the power relationships of the parties doing business together, are more equal. This point is also supported by Boardman's work in Chapter 11 in this book.

Grace Ann's Note

To summarize what we have presented in Part I, recall that we introduced the concept of "indigenous ways-of-knowing" because it is difficult to understand another culture without considering that culture's way of looking at the world and way of making sense of the world. Then we suggested Eight Aspects of Tribal Wisdom, the tribal values and practices that are especially relevant for the Euro-Western business world. This view of indigenous-style ethics was placed in a context of trends in studying business ethics. Indigenous ethics appears most compatible with a pragmatist perspective. Finally, we offer a four-quadrant model to focus on the different ethical concerns likely to emerge for businesses arising from and operating within the same culture versus those crossing cultural boundaries.

We conclude Part I with two case examples. First is the case of a business we classify as an "Elders" company based on Table 5.2. Mabel Sanchez presents the case of NOVA Corporation, a Native-owned corporation. Sanchez discusses how NOVA reflects six of the Eight Aspects of Tribal Wisdom: relationship, usefulness, trust, gifting, egalitarianism, and barter. Second is a Case Vignette of a business or group of businesses that we classify as "Traders" based on Table 5.2, the Laguna Development Corporation.

CASE EXAMPLE

NOVA Corporation

— Mabel Sanchez

Growing up in El Paso, Texas, I have always been in contact with tribes. For example, I have enjoyed the concerts at the Speaking Rock Entertainment Center located in the Ysleta Del Sur Pueblo. I have also frequented the Inn of the Mountain Gods resort and casino, and the Ski Apache ski resort in Ruidoso, New Mexico, land of the Mescalero Apache tribe. These businesses have evolved and renovated and are still running strong, demonstrating that Native Americans are successful business people.

Can businesses owned or operated by Native Americans practice traditional tribal values yet still compete successfully with Western businesses? NOVA Corporation would answer yes to this question. This answer will be explained in more detail below.

NOVA Corporation

This case example focuses on one of Dine-Development Corporation's (DDC) three subsidiaries, NOVA Corporation. NOVA's parent company DDC and its sister subsidiaries are 100 percent owned by the Navajo people. NOVA Corporation is an IT company that streamlines business processes while reducing the cost and complexity of the IT infrastructure (http://nova-dine.com/; accessed on March 11, 2016). In other words, they digitize and simplify daily business processes to make information and knowledge more accessible to people.

For the purpose of this case example, attention is given solely to NOVA Corporation. All subsidiaries, however, are equally important. In this case example, NOVA Corporation's activities and interactions will be analyzed to help explain why NOVA falls under the Elders' paradigm, and how it puts in practice the Eight Aspects of Tribal Wisdom.

Elders Story

In the storytelling model for cross-paradigm business ethics, NOVA Corporation falls under the Elders Story paradigm. As described earlier, Elders are experts in a service or process, and also, Elders usually incorporate tribal traditions into the way they do business. NOVA Corporation presents narratives of the Navajo history in its webpage, where a banner proclaims "Honoring our Past, Defining our Future." Interestingly, NOVA chooses to present certain narratives of the Navajo legacy. The narratives chosen are those that NOVA sees as inherently leading to the creation of NOVA Corporation.

History: Laying the Foundation for NOVA Corporation

In the NOVA Corporation webpage, under the tab "about us," there is an account of when the Navajo people were granted 3.5 million acres of land, in an area found within Utah, Arizona, and New Mexico. The Navajos were forcefully removed by the United States Army in 1864 and made the "Long Walk" of 300 miles to Bosque Redondo. In September 24, 1922, the Midwest Refining Company found oil in the Navajo reservation. This led to the creation of the Navajo government and Business Council, founded in 1922, to assist the Navajos with business affairs.

In 1933, the Navajo's traditional economy and social values were based on agriculture. This economy collapsed due to what was believed to be livestock overgrazing and eventual soil erosion on the reservation. The Bureau of Indian Affairs (BIA) commissioner's response to this situation was to reduce livestock holdings among the Navajo. This proved disastrous, leaving many Navajos further impoverished without their traditional sources of agricultural income.

Moreover, the BIA sold oil, coal, minerals, timber, and natural gas on Indian lands at below market prices and lacked effective accounting for these resources. The Navajo have recently been able to renegotiate this after lengthy court battles.

Later during World War II, in 1942, 29 Navajo military recruits reported to duty. They came to be known as the Navajo Code Talkers. These men developed the Navajo Code that replaced military terms, a code that could be transmitted and translated in 20 seconds. It was a code that could be transmitted through radio and telephone, and that the enemy was unable to decipher. This was a significant factor in the US winning the war. In September of 1992, the Navajo Code Talkers of World War II were honored at the Pentagon, in Washington DC, for their contribution to the United States' defense.

In 1984 the Navajo Nation and Business Council established a permanent trust fund. The fund received 12 percent of all revenue from the wealth of natural resources on the reservation. However, the trust fund revenues could not be utilized for the next twenty years, until 2004 (https://en.wikipedia.org/wiki/Navajo_Nation_Council; accessed on March 1, 2016).

In 2004, the DDC was created to diversify the Navajo Nation portfolio. As a result, NOVA Corporation was established in the same year, 2004. DDC currently holds three subsidiaries: NOVA Corporation, DDC-Construction Services LLC, and DDC-I.T. Services. The overarching mission of all three businesses is to ensure the continued economic development of the Navajo Reservation. These businesses compete successfully against non-Native business powerhouses. Their competitive advantage is their adherence to their legacy of culture and language (http://nova-dine.com/about-the-navajo; accessed on March 11, 2016).

The Navajo Code Talkers' historical contribution has helped shape NOVA Corporation. They carry on the legacy of the Navajo Code Talkers. NOVA, like the Code Talkers, encrypts data, and is entrusted with the protection of information on behalf of numerous organizations. As the Elders, NOVA carries the legacy of past ancestors and passes the wisdom through to present day people in a way that informs. Using the Elders' expertise, NOVA offers services to collect, analyze, and encrypt data, and provides the infrastructure to get the data safely to the rightful owner(s).

Now that we have reviewed the recent history of the Navajo Nation, we turn to the values and tribal traditions which characterize the way NOVA Corporation conducts business. The next sections describe how an emphasis on relationship, on usefulness rather than ownership, on trust, gifting, egalitarianism, and barter, all are traditional tribal values that characterize the operations of NOVA Corporation today.

Relationship

NOVA Corporation, driven by Navajo values, maintains a harmonious balance of relationships among humans and the planet (Cordova, 2007). For example, NOVA's mission to streamline business practices collaterally contributes to the health of the planet by digitizing processes. Thereby, the digitized processes require less paper and storage space reducing the amount of material and space waste.

Moreover, NOVA offers the Field Information Support Tool (FIST), which "is a commercial-off-the-shelf smartphone and web-based Knowledge Management System that advances the power of data fusion and knowledge creation for a wide variety of mission sets to include military, law enforcement, governance, and humanitarian missions" (http://nova-dine.com/solution/field-information-support-tool; accessed on March 1, 2016). In other words, NOVA Corporation offers their services through FIST, an application accessed through standard manufactured smartphones and tablets, rather than custom made technology. This allows customers to use their everyday smartphones and tablets, which translates to less e-waste and a decreased use of natural resources since new technology does not need to be manufactured.

NOVA proves to be very conscientious regarding the Navajo Nation and Mother Earth. Its actions to reduce the use of paper and raw materials demonstrate a great respect to its environment. And, the digitization of data allows more people to access data at once bridging people from around the world, encouraging communication and collaboration among people.

Usefulness

Traditional tribal value considers usefulness as important. Usefulness is the access to something and not ownership of it (Rosile & Boardman, 2011). NOVA's FIST was designed for both the commercial marketplace as well as for use under government contract. The Federal Acquisition Regulation (FAR) is a complex set of rules establishing the federal government's purchasing process (https://www.sba.gov/content/federal-acquisition-regulations-far; accessed on March 11, 2016), which is sometimes difficult for small businesses to comply with. NOVA

Corporation not only complies with the FAR but also offers services that help small businesses upgrade their systems to comply with the FAR requisites.

Moreover, NOVA's ties to its people, the Navajo, are always present through a series of efforts. For example, NOVA donated its services and provided Wi-Fi at the Navajo Nation Fair (http://nova-dine.com/nova-partners-to-bring-wifi-to-navajo-nation-fair; accessed on March 1, 2016), where the prospect of bringing Wi-Fi to the Navajo Nation Reservation was discussed. NOVA proves its usefulness by focusing on the straightforward access to its services and not on ownership (Rosile & Boardman, 2011).

Building Trust

Despite the problematic past between the Navajo Nation and the US government, NOVA Corporation has moved forward and now works closely with the US government. NOVA currently has five multimillion dollar contracts with the US government. These contracts include the resource management for the Veterans Affairs initiatives, ensuring that the Seaport-e community has reliable Wi-Fi connectivity and information while at sea, enhancing the current defense information system agency, and upgrading small businesses' IT needs in order to facilitate government contracting (http://nova-dine.com/contract-vehicles; accessed on March 11, 2016). Visibly, NOVA Corporation has the trust of the US government. NOVA's ability to encrypt and keep data safe, its ISO 9001:2008 certification, and its numerous contracts with the government are ways NOVA displays trust in itself and its customers.

Gifting Rather than Getting

NOVA Corporation was awarded Minority Business of the year in 2013, and American Indian Business of the year and fastest growing company in 2014 (http://www.ddc-dine.com/ddc-timeline/; accessed on March 1, 2016). Along with its immense success in less than ten years after being established, NOVA gives back to its Navajo community consistently. For example, to contribute to the Navajo Nation's economic prosperity, NOVA has awarded scholarships for many years to about 22 Navajo students (http://nova-dine.com/nova-awards-scholarships-to-navajo-students; accessed on March 1, 2016) every year.

In addition, refurbished laptops were donated to the Adolescent Care Unit, which houses youths of ages 13–17 with psychiatric and/or substance abuse issues. This effort provides a means for youths who have dropped out of school to reenter school and earn credits through an online recovery program (http://nova-dine.com/nova-donates-laptops-to-navajo-adolescent-care-unit;

accessed on March 1, 2016). Furthermore, NOVA Corporation fosters its employees' attitude of gifting rather than just gifting at the corporate level. For instance, employees donate portions of their paycheck to an organization of their choice. This past year, Navajo United Way was the recipient of employee donations (http://nova-dine.com/nova-donates-to-navajo-united-way; accessed on March 1, 2016). Therefore, not only does NOVA Corporation give back to its community, but also NOVA's employees can participate in giving back to their community.

Egalitarianism

Egalitarianism prevails in NOVA Corporation. This value is rooted in the Navajo Nation government, which its guiding principles are: Professionalism, Respect, Integrity, Culture and Tradition, and Equality.[1] One way the Navajo Nation government maintains egalitarianism is by providing 88 Council delegates, who represent the 110 Navajo Nation chapters, or communities. The Council delegates' job is not only to discuss critical issues and enact legislation but also to explain the policies and procedures to their chapter in the Navajo language, sometimes engaging elders to discuss policies and procedures from a traditional perspective (i.e., storytelling) (http://www.ongd.navajo-nsn.gov/Portals/0/Files/leader.pdf; p. 4; accessed on March 1, 2016).

Egalitarianism can also be seen in NOVA's efforts to provide high-end IT services to the Indian Country and not just the Navajo Nation. The Indian Country is made up of many self-governing communities throughout the United States. NOVA partnered with Apple Incorporated that allows NOVA Corporation to be the reseller of Apple products in Indian Country. The deal also gives Apple the opportunity to provide specialized technology training sessions to various Native American tribes (http://nova-dine.com/nova-expands-apple-reach; accessed on March 1, 2016).

NOVA is 100 percent Navajo owned but it believes in the advancement of the Indian Country as a whole, because all people on earth should have equal rights in it. For this, NOVA Corporation is dedicated to offering access to high-end IT services to all Indian Country citizens and not just the citizens of the Navajo Nation.

---

1. For brevity purposes, the Navajo's guiding principles are presented. However, for more information on the Diné Fundamental Laws and Bill of Rights visit http://www.ongd.navajo-nsn.gov/ (March 1, 2016).

Barter Economy

NOVA Corporation has created a barter economy with its interns. Every year, NOVA invests in two interns for a summer, providing skills and experience to enhance their opportunities in obtaining an incredible job. However, this comes with the expectation that these students will use those skills to help continue the development of the economy for the Navajo Nation. NOVA has plans of opening a training center in their Albuquerque office, providing career development and certifications to Navajo students (http://nova-dine. com/nova-educates-interns-from-the-navajo-nation; accessed on March 1, 2016). NOVA Corporation exchanges knowledge and experience for future creativity and innovation stemming from its people for its people.

Conclusion

NOVA Corporation prides itself of being in the people business delivering solutions. Its success against non-Native business powerhouses comes from NOVA's adherence to the legacy of the Navajo culture and language The way business is carried out in this corporation reveals most aspects of American Indian business-related traditional values and practices such as relationship, usefulness, trust, gifting, egalitarianism, and barter economy.

The Elders Story paradigm applies to NOVA Corporation for its service of encrypting data and making it accessible to those the data belongs to. They diffuse knowledge through data. Under this paradigm, the danger to businesses operating as Elders is in tribal values being eroded or overcome by the dominant profit-first culture, potentially leading to loss of market. However, NOVA's Navajo roots run deep through the company, and NOVA incorporates at least six (6) out of eight (8) Aspects identified in Chapter 1 as aspects of tribal wisdom most relevant for business ethics.

NOVA Corporation, as many other Native American businesses, is thriving. Its competitive advantage in the market is its culture, legacy, and language. NOVA Corporation is proof that a balanced relationship among humans and the planet does not go against company growth and success. On the contrary, the evidence in this case example demonstrates that following traditional tribal values is good for business, even in a high-tech contemporary business. NOVA's tribal values establish strong ties with not only the corporation and its community, but also between employees themselves and their community.

Search for Wisdom

— Dr. Grace Ann Rosile

1. Can you think of, or find on the Internet, other companies which demonstrate any of the six (6) tribal values we find in NOVA Corporation?
   Reminder: those values found in NOVA are relationship, usefulness
   rather than ownership, trust, gifting, egalitarianism, and barter.

   (Only two of the eight Aspects of Tribal Wisdom are missing in this
   case: Non-Acquisitiveness and Disclosure. This is only due to our limiting
   of case information to that which is publically available. NOVA may
   practice aspects of Non-Acquisitiveness and Disclosure, we simply do
   not have that information to say whether they do or do not apply to
   NOVA Corporation.)

2. Does NOVA appear to be a very different kind of corporation from
   most American companies? Is the difference more a matter of degree,
   because NOVA incorporates all six aspects of tribal wisdom, and to a
   greater degree than most US companies? Or is NOVA qualitatively different in who they are and how they conduct business?

3. Which of NOVA's six aspects of tribal wisdom do you think is most
   important to them?

4. Which of NOVA's six aspects of tribal wisdom would you most like to
   see other US companies emphasize more?

CASE VIGNETTE

Laguna Development Corporation

— Dr. Grace Ann Rosile

Laguna Development Corporation (LDC) is owned by the Pueblo of Laguna, located outside of Albuquerque, New Mexico. Founded in 1998, LDC has three casinos, two travel centers, and several retail businesses. LDC employees over 1000 employees and enjoys over $2million in annual revenues. It has had great success in a highly competitive local market, always meeting or exceeding annual financial goals.

Long-time President and CEO Mr. Jerald "Jerry" D. Smith is highly committed to operating LDC according to strong ethical beliefs so that both its operations and its financial successes contribute to the values and beliefs of the people of the Pueblo. Mr. Smith's father had been a religious leader within his tribe, so it is quite natural for him to be concerned that the businesses he leads are operating with great integrity and respect for tribal traditions.

In a speech at New Mexico State University, Mr. Smith emphasized the importance he placed on running LDC's businesses with high moral standards in harmony with the traditional values of the Pueblo of Laguna. In his personal management style, he likes to promote from within, building strong business relationships among his team. While turnover rates among casino executives are extremely high in the industry overall, he retains his executives through this upward mobility. In addition, he promises his executives that political changes in tribal governance will not threaten their jobs. With this approach, his turnover among casino managers is many times lower that of his competitors.

The following information was provided to me directly by email from Mr. Smith and his Senior Executive Admin Assistant Ms. Alysha Chavez.

LDC applies tribal ethics and values into the real world operation of our businesses on a daily basis, as follows:

1. Company Core Values are rooted in tribal values: Friendliness, Cleanliness, Dependability, High Integrity, and Wisdom.

2. Mission Statement reflects those values: We are a Laguna-owned business pursuing opportunities that improve and strengthen the Laguna

community and its economy. Through our high performance culture we provide unparalleled entertainment, extraordinary customer service and quality products. We honor our core values and with an enterprising spirit as we foster growth opportunities for the LDC family.

3. Though LDC is a separate legal entity from the Pueblo and is governed separately by an independent board of directors, we work in concert with tribal leaders to ensure our interests are parallel to achieve the social and economic objectives of the Pueblo and the corporation.

4. Employees of LDC, native and non-native, are directly engaged in activities that support the culture and tradition of Laguna Pueblo. LDC employees are directly engaged in plans and programs in education, health care, sports, the environment, and government programs and promotions where assistance can be provided.

5. LDC and its employees directly and indirectly support the traditions of the Pueblo in activities such as feast days, community clean-up days, Pueblo employee training and education.

6. LDC financial experts regularly consult with tribal officials to provide mutually beneficial information to ensure the economic vitality of tribal government and corporate finances.

7. LDC and the Pueblo of Laguna have a long-standing cash sharing agreement in place whereby financial resources are contributed to tribal government in a formula that ensures mutual confidence and stability over the long term.

8. The ethics and values of Laguna Pueblo are embedded into the everyday operation of the company by virtue of the fact that 52% of our employees are Laguna tribal members or members of other tribes.

Search for Wisdom

— Dr. Grace Ann Rosile

1. Go to http://www.lagunadevcorp.com/laguna-development-corporation. aspx to find out more about Laguna Development Corporation.[2] Do they have any job openings for which you might have an interest?

2. In what ways do LDC's human resources policies reflect the values of the Pueblo of Laguna?

3. Do you think that LDC has more, less, or about the same amount of involvement in community activities as other non-tribal business with which you are familiar? Why do you think this is so?

Grace Ann's note

Many thanks to Mabel Sanchez for her NOVA Corporation case example! And many thanks to Mr. Jerry Smith and Ms. Alysha Chavez for the information they provided for the case vignette on Laguna Development Corporation. This concludes Part I.

Next, in Part II, we look at indigenous storytelling as its own way of making sense of the world, and also, as the favored way used by American Indian tribes to convey moral lessons. We begin with a transcription of a story told by Dr. Gregory Cajete to a group at New Mexico State University during the making of the Tribal Wisdom film series. This is a story of Coyote and Raven, two "trickster" characters who are often featured in tribal stories.

---

2. The Laguna Development Corporation web site, at http://www.lagunadevcorp.com/laguna-development-corporation.aspx, and personal correspondence from Mr. Jerry Smith and Ms. Alysha Chavez of LDC.

References

Aristotle (350 BC/1954). *Aristotle: Rhetoric and Poetics*. Introduction by Friedrich Solmsen; *Rhetoric* translated by W. Rhys Roberts; *Poetics* translated by Ingram Bywater. New York, NY: The Modern Library (Random House).

Bakhtin, M. M. (1990). *Art and Answerability*. In M. Holquist & V. Liapunov (Eds.). Translation and Notes by Vadim Liapunov; supplement translated by Kenneth Brostrom. From Bakhtin's first published article and his early 1920s notebooks. Austin, TX: University of Texas Press.

Bakhtin, M. M. (1993). *Toward a Philosophy of the Act*. In M. Holquist & V. Liapunov (Eds.). Translation and Notes by Vadim Liapunov. From Bakhtin's early 1920s notebooks. First English printing in 1993. Austin, TX: University of Texas Press.

Bentham, J. (1987). *An introduction to the principles of morals and legislation*. Amherst, NY: Prometheus.

Claw, C. M., Verbos, A. K., Rosile, G. A. (2017 forthcoming). Business Ethics and Native American values. chapter In D. M. Kennedy, C. Harrington, A. K. Verbos, D. Stewart, J. S. Gladstone, & G. Clarkson (Eds.). *American Indian business: A reader*. Seattle, WA: Status: Contract with University of Washington Press. Submitted to publisher.

Cordova, V. F. (2007). Against the singularity of the human species. In K. D. Moore, K. Peters, T. Jojola, & A. Lacy (Eds.). *How it is: The native American philosophy of V. F. Cordova*. Tucson, AZ: University of Arizona Press.

Dewey, J. (1920). Americanism and Localism. *The Dial, 68*(6), 684–688.

Dewey, J. (1938). *Logic: The theory of inquiry*. New York, NY: Holt, Rinehart, and Winston.

Gilligan, C. (1982). *In a different voice: Psychological theory and women's development*. Cambridge, MA: Harvard University Press.

Gladstone, J. S. (2012). *Old Man and Coyote barter: An inquiry into the spirit of a Native American philosophy of business* (Order No. 3537767, New Mexico State University). ProQuest Dissertations and Theses, 284 pages.

Gladstone, J. S., & Claw, C. (2015). CMS Division Case Competition Finalist: *Dark Side Case: Trickster Devices – Misappropriating Cultural Capital*. Academy of Management Meeting, Vancouver, BC, August 7–11.

Held, V. (2006). *The ethics of care: Personal, political and global*. New York, NY: Oxford University Press.

Kant, I. (1785/2002). Groundwork for the Metaphysics of morals *(A. J. Wood, Trans.).* New Haven, CT: Yale University Press. (German 1785, English translation 2002).

Mill, J. S. (1861). In A. Ryan (Ed.), *Utilitarianism and other essays.* London: Penguin Books/Viking (1987).

Rawls, J. (1971/1999). *A theory of justice.* Oxford: Harvard University Press/Oxford University Press.

Rosile, G. A. (2014). American Indian Tribal Wisdom: A Storytelling Model for Cross-Paradigm Business Ethics. In *proceedings of the international association of cross-cultural communication in management.* University of Warwick, 26–28 June.

Rosile, G. A., & Boardman, C. (2011). Antenarrative Ethics of Native American Indian Trading. In *proceedings of the standing conference for management and organizational inquiry*, Philadelphia, PA.

Verbos, A. K., Kennedy, D. M., & Claw, C. M. (2016). Native American values applied to leadership and business ethics education. In G. A. Rosile (Ed.), *Tribal wisdom for business ethics.* Bingley, UK: Emerald Group Publishing Limited.

Part II
Storytelling and Indigenous Pedagogies for Business Ethics

A Coyote Story for Business Ethics Pedagogy

Gregory Cajete

There are many stories that involve animals which are used to show the various kinds of relationships in this web of all life. These stories many times have a moral, and that moral is presented in mostly very humorous and also very contextual ways.

I'm reminded of one story, about the ability to see something. It comes essentially from Plains Indians cultures, with variations of it in Cheyenne and Lakota. It is a story of Coyote.

This story begins with coyote going along, and coyotes have a tendency to want to look at everything. And they look at details, and they're always looking at different kinds of features in the landscape. And they're always looking for food, because they're always hungry.

And so coyote is going along and he's looking for food, and he bumps into a tree. And in the tree there is a raven, a raven that sees that this crazy coyote bumped into this tree, he's almost knocked me out of this tree, and this is my tree. And of course the coyote uses some very defamatory language and says "Well I don't care! This is my space and I'm going to use it the way I want to!"

And then the raven says "I notice that you're looking for food. And you know what, the best way to look for food is to just pluck your eyes out and hold them in front of you, so you can see further. And then you can see around you, and above you." And so coyote being coyote and being so zealous in finding food, plucks his eyes out.

And he starts to use his eyes to look in different places. But he bumps into the tree again. And this time, as he bumps into the tree, his eyes fall out of his hands and they go rolling around. So all of a sudden he's blind, because he's lost his eyes.

And so he begins groping, groping, and groping, and he keeps bumping into the tree and falling down. And of course raven is just laughing at him, because Raven tricked him into taking his eyes out, and teaching him a lesson that you have to have an understanding of the whole, as much as you have to have an understanding of the detail. That's kind of the big moral, or the lesson.

Eventually Raven tells him where his eyes have rolled, where to find his eyes. But he makes Coyote pay dearly for that information. And I think that lesson is a really good lesson for the way we tend to operate in the world where we look at the details ad infinitum, but we forget about the whole.

We forget about our impact, as we move around looking for food, looking for sustenance, looking for "business" if you will. And so I think that that tale really epitomizes the situation that we tend to find ourselves in, as we look at these very complex formulas for doing business, which are very detailed. We forget about the impact of that action, the impact on society as well as the impact on all the other life forms as seen through the indigenous world view.

Implications of Storytelling for Business Ethics Pedagogy

Telling stories like this one about Coyote is the traditional way in which tribal peoples have conveyed cultural values and taught moral lessons. "Story, through the oral tradition, becomes both a source of content and methodology for indigenous community education" (Cajete in Eder & Holyan, 2010, p. ix) and further, "Indigenous teaching is essentially rooted in the structure and active-verb-based process of creating and living through story" (Cajete in Eder & Holyan, 2010, p. xi).

The lessons provided by indigenous storytelling are deeply embedded in rich context. This storytelling engages the imagination and the unconscious, and is a cocreated process between teller and listener, student and teacher. Unfortunately we have lost some of that storytelling awareness and skill which was an integral part of tribal cultures and oral traditions. This is why I have said elsewhere:

> The legacy and the innate learning potential of indigenous *storying* must be recaptured and made an integral part of contemporary education at every level … . The difference between the transfer of knowledge in modern Western education and that of indigenous education is that information has been separated from the stories and presented as data, description, theory, and formula. Modern students are left for the most part to re-contextualize the information within a story. The problem is that, for the most part, students have not been conditioned by modern culture or education to re-contextualize this information. Their natural sense for story has been schooled out of them, so they do not know how to mobilize their imagination to interact with the content with which they are presented—they have lost their innate awareness of story … . Making story the basis of teaching and learning provides one of the best ways to do this kind of contextualizing and enhancing of meaning in all areas of content. (Cajete in Eder & Holyan, 2010, pp. xii–xiii)

The Coyote story I told is about how many times people focus so closely on the details that they forget about the whole picture.

They don't have a sense of those impacts that their behavior or words or actions may have, with regard to that greater or larger goal. I think that many times business is like the coyote.

Grace Ann's Note

Many thanks to Dr. Gregory Cajete for his telling of this story! The story of Coyote and Raven is a high-context traditional story. But traditionally, storytellers did not tell the "lesson" or "moral of the story." However, today, not all listeners of the story are as aware of this context as may have been in the past. Because of this loss of some of our previous implicit understanding of context, Dr. Cajete gave some "hints" about the meaning of the story.

Next, Dr. David Boje explains the deep differences between indigenous storytelling and Euro-Western storytelling by using his concepts of antenarrative and living story.

Reference

Eder, D., & Holyan, R. (2010). *Life lessons through storytelling: Children's exploration of ethics*. Bloomington, IN: Indiana University Press.

But that's Not a Story! Antenarrative Dialectics Between and Beneath Indigenous Living Story and Western Narratives

David M. Boje

Tribal Wisdom has two important lessons to teach Western narratology. First, indigenous storytelling is living story with sociomateriality in the space, time, and mattering of flux of everything's energy waves, including our own. These elements of space, time, and matter are inseparable in quantum storytelling and also in IWOK so we use the term *spacetimemattering*. Second, sociomateriality of everything is both spiritual and ecological, in "*spiritual ecology.*" Here, the quantum storytelling community is split with half treating *spacetimemattering* as spiritless, and half favoring *spiritual ecology* as found in IWOK. This chapter contributes to an understanding of differences between indigenous and living story in contrast with Western narrative. Western narrative contains more socially constructed narratives of separation such as we find in Western sustainability development, with its separation of human life from plant, animal, and planet life. This is in contrast to the sociomateriality of IWOK, including Native American wisdom rooted in the connectedness and dynamism of Native Science and spiritual ecology.

How Living Story and Indigenous Story are Antenarrative Aspects of Storytelling

Stories and Sensemaking — All storytelling is not the same. On hearing an indigenous story told in the traditional way, the listener not raised with such traditions would have difficulty understanding the meaning of this type of story. Some of us would say "This is not a story." Basso (1996) recounts some of the stories of the Western Apache, which no one but a cultural insider would understand, or would even recognize as a story.

Keep in mind also, that many American Indians have not had the opportunity to be raised in traditional ways in a traditional tribal community. Given the misguided attempts to eradicate Indianness in colonial times (some of which survive to this day), we are fortunate to have what we do. Even in the communities that survive, traditions and cultural contexts may change over time.

The effect of all these changes is that our story listeners are not the same, and sometimes, in response to these changes, the storytelling also is modified. More specifically, indigenous storytelling may be somewhat less contextualized and less non-linear than it was in the past. Gregory Cajete commented on this in a personal conversation about his own storytelling. He suggested that given the changes of modern times, tribal storytellers would incorporate more "hints" as to the meaning of traditional stories in their storytelling.

This chapter explains some differences between what is commonly called "storytelling" in the Euro-Western tradition, and the very different style of storytelling which is the tradition of American Indian tribal peoples. The reason many of these traditional tribal stories may not "make sense" to outsiders is due in part to their highly contextualized nature. Adding to the mystery is the non-linear ways-of-knowing and ways of constructing stories among many indigenous cultures.

In Chapter 8, Rosile describes some of these differences between indigenous and Euro-Western storytelling practices. The focus there in Chapter 8 is more on the different practices. Here in this chapter, the focus is on some of the underlying reasons why those differences came to exist, and how a story is constructed, or how it comes to be a story. The term for this is "antenarrative" (Boje, 2008; Boje, Haley, & Saylors, 2015). It is "ante" or before-the-story. It is also an "ante" or a bet on the direction or outcome of the story.

To assist in following the discussion of storytelling theories, I offer the following list of terms (Table 7.1). For each term, I provide a brief working definition relating to how these terms are used in this chapter. Some definitions and descriptions of these terms will also appear in the text. I am risking repetition for the sake of clarity, especially for those unfamiliar with this perspective on storytelling.

Now that we have a base line of terms, the first term to put into context, and into relationship with the other terms, is "antenarrative." To explain antenarrative, three terms are important to understand. First is "BME." The BME is a story structured with a beginning, middle, and end, usually in a linear fashion. A leads to B leads to C. The BME story is what we think of when those of us from Euro-Western cultural traditions think of a "story."

The second term is "living story." The living story is the life that was occurring before we made it into a story. It is the lived experience before we made sense of our life experiences by telling those experiences as a story to ourselves and/or to others.

The third term is "indigenous storytelling." Indigenous storytelling tends to be non-linear, without a clear BME, highly contextualized, more flexible and dynamic, and less petrified into "the" story. These differences between Western narrative and indigenous and living story are summarized in Table 7.2.

The antenarrative is what happens when the lived experience of living story begins to form as an indigenous story or a

Table 7.1: Terms of Storytelling Theory.

Term	Definition
1. Storytelling	a general term that includes the entanglement of relationships of narrative, living story, and their particular antenarrative connections and transformations.
Story	the broad-level, all-encompassing term for story fragments and various forms of story of immediate lived experience; a subset of storytelling.
2. Narrative	as a subset of storytelling, it is a particular form of abstract events and characterizations, which is recognizable as a plot.
3. Antenarrative	what happens before, beneath, bets on future, the becoming and between the lived experience (living story web) and what becomes packaged as a narrative, whether BME (see below) or non-linear.
4. BME narrative	a linear pot which is recognized as an abstraction because it has a clear beginning, middle, and end, often along with various identifiable plots and characters.
5. Living Story Web	immediate lived experiences which are swirling around before they have been shaped into plots and abstract themes by acts of narrative. (See Table 7.2.)
6. Indigenous Story	a (living) story without a clear BME, with non-human characters, and without the coherence of plot one expects of narrative. (See Table 7.2.)

Table 7.1: (*Continued*)

Term	Definition
7. Quantum Storytelling	reflects the interconnectedness of all quanta (energy) existence in the *spacetimemattering*; quanta views everything as a form of energy. Although some do not, I see this energy as having a living Spirit that centers in its material existence.
8. Fractiles	repeating patterns of self-sameness across various scales of magnifications, which may appear in stories or narratives.
9. Animism/Vitalism	Animism is considered by western science to be anthropomorphism, but in indigenous wisdom, the mountains, rivers, rocks, and fire, all the elements of Nature, including every plant and animal, have living energy. Vitalism, on the other hand, in quantum materialism, has the quanta (living energy) of waves that can collapse into particle formations.
10. Spacetimemattering	a term by Barad (2003, 2007) is the inseparabilty, the very entanglement of space, time, and mattering. I use it to look at how storytelling is spatializing, temporalizing, and mattering in existential ways.
11. IWOK	Indigenous Ways-of-Knowing
12. Spiritual Ecology	concept by Cajete (2000) that refers to the Spirits of the world, of which we are a part, and from the quanta to the cosmos the ways of living energy.

Table 7.2: Comparison of Storytelling Genres.

	Euro-Western Narrative	Indigenous and Living Story
Structure	BME Beginning, Middle, and End; may be Linear or Cyclic	Without beginning or end; in the middle; spiral and rhizomatic assemblages
Time Orientation	Time is subjective, focus is on an unchanging view of "the" past	Time folds on itself; Present-oriented with backshadows of the past as the past mixes with present to provide lessons for the future
Place Orientation	Incidental and usually not important to the plot; or is an abstraction	Place is of central importance, it provides context and materiality and holds the story
Characters	Are human and restricted to participants in the plot	Includes humans, non-humans, and material objects as active participants, whether living, non-living or deceased, all in changing webs of relationships
Plot	Has a problem to solve, or question to answer, or mystery to resolve	Dynamic Being and Becoming; Revolves around relationships more than issues/plots/problems; highlights questions not answers
Past, present, or future orientation	Retrospective	Both in-the-moment and long term, through the generations, both retrospective and prospective

Source: Adapted from Rosile and Boje (2013).

Euro-Western BME story. In this process, the story begins to take shape as one of four (4) potential story structures: linear, cyclical, spiral, or rhizomatic assemblage (like a network).

Next, our antenarrative may become an indigenous story or a Euro-Western story. There are as many definitions of Euro-Western narrative as there are narratologists (Boje, 2014). I have found at least 30 definitions, and find little overlap, except for the assumptions of the separation of the sensemaking mind from the things that are inanimate. However, this common feature of separation is the very thing that makes most definitions of narrative unable to get at the actual nature of indigenous living story.

Indigenous story falls within what I call "living story." Indigenous storytelling carries quite different assumptions of reality from Euro-Western narrative and story. These assumptions include: the interconnection of all things, the animate nature and spiritual energy of all things, and the need for sustainable communities with high ecological literacy.

Rather than attempt to place indigenous storytelling within a typology of Western narrative definitions, I propose to look at Tribal Wisdom as its own category, on its own storytelling of IWOK terms. This approach requires a refusal to reduce storytelling to a duality between subjects and objects, or between People and Planet, embracing instead the living story nature of indigenous and American Indian wisdom, including the interfusion of sociomaterial forces with spiritual ecology.

Living Stories — Living Stories are in space/place, in time, and in mattering, *spacetimemattering*. As Cajete (2015, p. 96) puts it "Indigenous stories relate the experience of life lived in time and place" (p. 96). We are "storied and storying beings" and it is time to change the "story line"; "changing story lines of dysfunctional to ones of functionality, moving towards health" (p. 96). Those stories of life in harmony and balance and health "have deep roots" in the very "heart of the human psyche" and "the geography of the human soul" (p. 96).

One lives their living story in a web of living stories (Boje, 2001, 2008). The challenge is that many people are living their living stories with story lines that are unsustainable, lack a holistic context, and lack a story-frame with an ecological meaning. Not just humans tell stories. As James (1907/2008, p. 97) says, "things tell a story." Things have vitalism (Bennett, 2010).

Spiritual ecology is a bridge to my own work in "quantum storytelling" where people are bundles of energy; all things are energy waves, in the moving spirit of spiritual ecology in *spacetimemattering*. Vitalism in Western narratives of quantum physics does equate to spiritual ecology. Much of the work in quantum physics sociomateriality, *spacetimemattering*, is spiritless (see Boje, 2014 for a review of quantum physics and quantum metaphysics approaches).

In Cajete's Native Science, in tribal and community storytelling, there cannot be a separation between humanity, spirituality, nature, sociality, and materiality (Cajete, 2000). By contrast, in western narratology these many definitions focus on the linguistic turn, relying on social construction for meaning-making. This gives primacy to language, and furthers the separation of language from materiality. Attempts to bridge this separation are marginalized with a dismissive gesture to animal and plant spirits as forms of "animism." We must take a more open-minded approach to indigenous living story in its own right.

Indigenous and living story offers an alternative conception of storytelling where we are all created from and by the materiality process of storytelling. Further, indigenous storytelling is apt to give primacy to spirituality in natured sociomaterial processes where everything is flux and energy waves that have recurring patterns of renewal that we are complicit in sustaining, such as ecology held in trust for the seventh generation.

LittleBear (2000) in his introduction to Cajete's (2000) book, *Native Science: Natural Laws of Interdependence*, gives us an understanding of what I have been calling "quantum storytelling" (Boje, 2014; Boje & Henderson, 2014). Quantum storytelling is an embodied way of understanding ourselves, others, and the ecosystem. It shares something important with Native American science ways of living story ecology. "Native science is born of a lived and storied participation with the natural landscape" (Cajete, 2000, p. 2).

Native American Science inscribes ideas of "constant motion and flux, existence consisting of energy waves, interrelationships, all things being animate, space/place, renewal, and all thing being imbued with spirit" (LittleBear, 2000, p. x). The world is in motion, constant flux, and all things are undergoing processes of transformation, deformation, and restoration. This results in "'spider web' networks of relationships" where everything is interrelated, and the energy waves and "spirit" are the same thing (Para.: p. x).

"Everything in creation consists of a unique combination of energy waves" and material things are "simply the manifestation of a unique combination of energy waves" (LittleBear, 2000, pp. x–xi). This Native Science way of understanding the meaning of reality is consistent with advances in quantum physics. LittleBear goes on to point out that Native American Science detects "certain regular patters" of renewal and transformation of "seasons, migration of animals, or cosmic movement" (p. xi.).

In Henderson and Boje (2015) and Boje (2015a, 2015b) we look at how fractal patterns of renewal and transformation occur throughout existence, what LittleBear calls "cycles of plant life, seasons, and cosmic movements [that] are detected from particular spatial location that are sacred medicine sites" (LittleBear, 2000, p. xi). Fractals are repeating patterns of self-sameness across various scales of magnifications.

Quantum Storytelling therefore shares with Native American Science the search for meaning in the constant flux of energy waves of body, Earth, and cosmos. These fractal regularities, such as cycles of renewal and transformation, are however subject to change. Change comes from the action and inaction of humans, their technologies, and relationship to Earth. Many changes are not so desirable, such as climate change, deforestation, desertification, soil degradation, and water and air pollution.

"Storytelling is a very important aspect of Native America. It is not just the history but the actual living of the story … its livingness and spirit" in an "ecology, relational network of plants, animals, the land, and the cosmos" (LittleBear, 2000, p. xii). This is what my colleagues and I have been calling "living story web of interrelationships" in the *spacetimemattering* of quantum storytelling

(Henderson & Boje, 2014). Quantum storytelling, as used here, is the discovery of regular patterns of energy waves in the interrelationship of all things, and in ways that are consistent with spiritual ecology. There are other versions of quantum physics and storytelling, which omit spiritual, and focus just on the intra-activity of materiality *with* discourse (e.g., Barad, 2007).

Indigenous living story builds knowledge and wisdom around "ecological sustainability" models of community that "lay foundations for ecological literacy" (Cajete, 2015, p. 18). "Indigenous teaching is essentially rooted in the storied structure and process of storytelling. Story has been a primary way for us to connect different generations" (p. 106).

What are the ways in which quantum storytelling, and Native Science living story liveliness of eco-spiritual understanding differs from Western narrative? The assumptions that we are all energy beings, constellated by energy waves, in constant change and transformation in the inseparability of *spacetimemattering*, which is thoroughly spiritual, are quite different from the Western narrative paradigm. Indigenous storytelling is a way to "remember to remember who we are, where we have come from, and where we can go" (p. 106). In living story web, "communities can be thought of as complexes of stories, thoroughly interconnected and constantly interacting" (Cajete, 2015, p. 107). It is this sense of entanglement that for me defines quantum storytelling (Boje, 2014).

In sum, the "storytellers and story makers" (Cajete, 2015, p. 98) have different spiritual (and dispirited) standpoints. The discipline of storytelling is divided, as the history of colonization of IWOK gives witness. Cajete suggests four steps to take to preserve and revitalize Indigenous storytelling ways (Cajete, 2015, p. 98):

1. Go to the source of the stories, the place of the stories, the place of the people storying.

2. Build storying muscles by exercising the creative process of storytelling. In Indigenous storytelling, linear plotlines are avoided, and there are not tidy endings. Rather, the story teller and story listener rely on contextual clues, such as omitted details about place, history, the way one plants, how

one stalks game, and so on. Creatively thinking through the silent sides of a story (unspoken, yet implied) is a way to build story muscles.

3. Apply story lessons to living story, to living one's own story.

4. The survival of a community (or tribe) means resisting colonization of IWOK.

Transmotion — One example is Gerald Vizenor's transmotion. Vizenor's (2008) *Survivance: Narratives of Native Presence* has a focus on transmotion. Native transmotion is defined by Madsen (2008) as "an original natural union in the stories of emergence and migration that relate humans to an environment and to the spiritual and political significance of animals and other creations" (p. 70). The monotheism of western narrative, by contrast, "is dominance over natural reason, and native creation of other creatures" (*ibid.*).

Columbus imposed on tribal people the pronouns ("I") over "we," and a static territory on material-mythic-visionary movements and wandering of tribal people in spiritual nature (p. 70). Native storytelling and stories, for Vizenor (2008, p. 221), reflect the movements and mobilities in and between tribes, something that colonizers could not abide, forcing and disciplining tribes into static, discrete territories, and blood purity. The result is isolation, homelessness, and alienation.

Survival in a world riven by western narrative sense of place (static), time (retrospective), and materiality (objective removed from subjective) has to be subversive. This is why Vizenor draws upon Michel De Certeau's concept of tactical mobility, in his survivance message, as a way to disguise living stories within the culture of western narrative.

In Vizenor and Seaver (1993) *Narrative Chance*, the trickster is a character who does not remove contradiction, fragmentation, or multiplicities from the world, but rather holds these differences in balance (Madsen, 2008, pp. 67–68). The significance of these and other stories of Native Wisdom have been lost by the "wordies" (or Europeans), those western narratologists privileging coherence, integration, and the monologic of spoken or textual discourse in their desire to appropriate Trickster stories and reduce them to narrative.

We never had any trouble remembering to use plural pronouns, but most wordies could not understand who we were talking about. They saw the old woman but not the bear. We are one and the same. There's a trickster in the use of words that includes the natural world, a world according to the we in our metaphor in the wanaki game. (Vizenor & Seaver, 1993, *Dead Voices*, p. 39)

Search for Wisdom

— Dr. Grace Ann Rosile

1. How might you use the opening story at the start of this volume (Russell Means' grandfather's story), or a story like it, to strengthen what Greg Cajete calls "story muscles"?

2. How might the use of the words "I" and "we" affect a sense of separation of the Euro-Western peoples from the natural world?

3. Is the "I-We" of indigenous peoples an answer to Buber's "I-thou" critique? I interpret Buber as saying that modern alienation and despair are rooted in the modern (Euro-Western) habit of looking at everything we experience in the world as an "it" to be observed from a distance, rather than a "thou" to be encountered and loved. Do you agree? If so, does Vizenor's "I-We" answer that concern?

Grace Ann's Note

Many thanks to Dr. David Boje for explaining how deep differences in the way we tell a story affects how we make sense of our lived experiences. Next, I discuss some common practices in telling American Indian traditional morality tales intended to teach ethical lessons.

References

Barad, K. (2003). Posthumanist performativity: Toward an understanding of how matter comes to matter. *Journal of Women in Culture and Society*, *28*(3), 801–831.

Barad, K. (2007). *Meeting the universe halfway: Quantum physics and the entanglement of matter and meaning*. Durham, NC: Duke University Press.

Basso, K. H. (1996). *Wisdom sits in places: Landscape and language among the Western Apache*. Albuquerque, NM: UNM Press.

Bennett, J. (2010). *Vibrant matter: A political ecology of things*. Durham, NC: Duke University Press.

Boje, D. M. (2001). *Narrative methods for organizational and communication research*. London: Sage.

Boje, D. M. (2008). *Storytelling organizations*. London: Sage.

Boje, D. M. (2014). *Storytelling organizational practices: Managing in the quantum age*. London: Routledge.

Boje, D. M. (2015a). *Change solutions to the chaos of standards and norms overwhelming organizations: Four wings of tetranormalizing*. London: Routledge.

Boje, D. M. (2015b). Mapping quantum storytelling fractal patterns before and beneath triple bottom line's and veterans administration's stupid narratives. *Proceedings of big story conference*, December 17–19, 2015, Los Angeles, CA.

Boje, D. M., Haley, U., & Saylors, R. (2015). Antenarratives of organizational change: The microstoria of Burger King's storytelling in space, time and strategic context. *Human Relations Journal*, published online before print September 29, 2015. doi: 10.1177/0018726715585812. Retrieved from http://hum.sagepub.com/content/early/2015/09/24/0018726715585812.full.pdf?ijkey=twqfHIAyxnoC8DW&keytype=finite

Boje, D. M., & Henderson, T. (Eds.). (2014). *Being quantum: Ontological storytelling in the age of antenarrative*. Cambridge: Cambridge Scholars Press.

Cajete, G. (2000). *Native science: Natural laws of interdependence*. Santa Fe, NM: Clear Light Publishers.

Cajete, G. A. (2015). *Indigenous community: Rekindling the teachings of the seventh fire*. St. Paul, MN: Living Justice Press.

Henderson, T., & Boje, D. M. (2015). *Organizational development and change theory: Managing fractal organizing processes*. London: Routledge.

James, W. (1907/2008). *Pragmatism – A series of lectures by William James, 1906–1907*. Rockville, MD: Arc Manor.

LittleBear, L. (2000). Introduction. In Cajete (Ed.), *Native science: Natural laws of interdependence*. Santa Fe, NM: Clear Light Publishers.

Madsen, D. L. (2008). Rereading trauma through *The Heirs of Columbus* and *The Crown of Columbus*. In G. Vizenor (Ed.), *Survivance: Narratives of native presence*. Lincoln, NE: University of Nebraska.

Rosile, G. A., & Boje, D. (2013). Critical postmodern: The antenarrative wagering of native American Indians under material conditions of intercultural multiplicity. In M. Marchiori (Ed.) *Faces of cultures and communication*. Brazil: Conselho Nacional de Desenvolvimento Cientifico e Tecnológico no diretório dos Grupos de Pesquisa do Brasil.

Vizenor, G. (Ed.). (2008). *Survivance: Narratives of native presence*. Lincoln, NE: University of Nebraska Press.

Vizenor, G., & Seaver, J. E. (1993). *Narrative chance: Postmodern discourse on Native American Indian literatures*. (American Indian Literature and Critical Studies Series). Norman, OK: University of Oklahoma Press.

So, What Does it Mean? Mysterious Practices of Indigenous Storytellers

Grace Ann Rosile

Both Native Americans and Euro-Westerners use stories to convey moral lessons. However, Native American Storytelling is very different from Euro-Western storytelling traditions. In this chapter, I discuss these differences, and suggest ways the Euro-Western world might adapt and adopt indigenous storytelling methods, especially when storytelling is used to impart a moral lesson.

I begin with a story which might sound like an indigenous story at first, but it is different in several significant ways. I offer an alternative "indigenized" version of the story to demonstrate those differences. I conclude with ways to adapt your own storytelling to be more indigenous-like by using the "5 I's" of indigenous storytelling methods.

The Little Bird: A Euro-Western Morality Tale

(Adapted from Rosile, Pepion, & Gladstone, 2012, used with permission)

A little bird was flying south for the winter. It was so cold the bird froze and fell to the ground into a large field.

While he was lying there, a cow came by and dropped some dung on him.

As the frozen bird lay there in the pile of cow dung, he began to realize how warm he was.

The dung was actually thawing him out!

He lay there all warm and happy, and soon began to sing for joy.

A passing cat heard the bird singing and came to investigate.

Following the sound, the cat discovered the bird under the pile of cow dung, and promptly dug him out, and then ate him.

There are 3 morals to this story:

(1) Not everyone who poops on you is your enemy.

(2) Not everyone who gets you out of poop is your friend.

(3) And when you're in deep poop, it's best to keep your mouth shut!

(*Note*: The Little Bird story is taken from Rosile, *et al.*, 2012; Jan 2012 DFEI Conference Presentation, Hotel Encanto, Las Cruces, NM; presentation entitled "Daniels Principles of Business Ethics and Tribal Ethics: Using Indigenous Methods of Storytelling to Convey Moral Principles" available on the Internet and used with permission. There are many versions of The Little Bird story. One version comes from the 1973 Sergio Leone movie "My Name is Nobody." The current version was forwarded to Rosile by a student many years ago, author unknown.)

The story of "The Little Bird" is humorous, yet is an example of the Euro-Western type of storytelling used to convey a moral lesson. The most obvious difference between this morality tale and indigenous stories for ethics education is that with this story you are told the meaning or the "moral of the story." However, there are many more ways, perhaps not so obvious, in which traditional indigenous stories differ from Euro-Western ones.

Below are seven factors specifically related to indigenous-style storytelling for ethics education. Indigenous stories are more:

1. Terse

2. Cryptic

3. Sacred

4. Participative

5. Place-oriented

6. Time-bending

7. Non-human-centric

UNIVERSITY OF WINCHESTER LIBRARY

1. Terse: Many Native American stories are highly contextualized and give the "bare bones" while leaving the details for the listener to imagine. This makes the story more participative, drawing in the listener as a cocreator of the tale.

Native American stories emerge from IWOK. Indigenous science (Cajete, 2000) prefers observation to manipulation, and seeks integration and interdependence rather than separation and control. The focus is on the whole rather than the parts. This leads to stories which are highly contextualized. Highly contextualized stories, in the extreme, can become what Boje (2001, 2008) calls "terse." For example, in a factory with a history of labor-management strife, workers knew the story of a union activist who was forced to quit by management. The activist's health was poor, and management assigned him a job which required climbing a lot of stairs each day. The man had to quit to preserve his health. For years afterwards, any time management was felt to be retaliating against troublesome union supporters, workers would say to that person, "You'll be walking the stairs!" The phrase was all that was needed to signify the whole story of that long-ago event.

With indigenous stories, the rich context provides much missing detail. Further, the listener is free to fill in those details on their own. For example, stock characters like Coyote and Raven have traits that were already known to tribal listeners in the past. In current times, not even all tribal people are familiar with some traditional tribal artifacts like the character of Coyote. For this reason, as Cajete has noted elsewhere in this volume, indigenous storytellers in current times may be less terse, and may provide more "hints" about the meaning of a story.

2. Cryptic: The "moral" of the story is either not readily apparent, or multiple "morals" exist. This allows the listener the freedom to interpret the meaning for themselves, rather than be told "the" meaning by the teller. Wisdom must be sought, it is not taught.

Indigenous storytelling, like indigenous science (Cajete, 2000), is non-linear. This non-linearity appears confusing to our predominantly linear Euro-Western ways of thinking. This also contributes to the frequent reaction of linear thinkers of "Get to the point!" Linear thinkers expect the facts to line up and lead to "the" point. Non-linearity means there may be many points, and the so-called facts do not necessarily lead directly to those points. This adds to the cryptic appearance of non-linear indigenous stories.

Fixico (2003) quotes noted Indian activist Russell Means (in Means with Wolf, 1995, p. 18):

> Grandpa John told me endless stories about young men who had opportunities to live up to their names. One day, he said, "there was a young man named Looks Twice—really, he was more like a boy—who left his village alone to hunt, hoping to bring back some meat. He wanted to prove that he was a man. It was in the springtime. He went without a bow or a lance, and he killed a deer with his knife." … "How did he kill the deer, Grandpa?" I interrupted. "You'd better figure that out," he said. "That's what will make you a man." (p. 88)

3. Sacred: Stories, according to Boje (2001, 2008), are the life's blood of a culture. They are treated with greatest respect. Protocols exist regarding who has the right to tell a story, and when a story can and cannot be told. For example, some stories are told only during winter, when people are not so fully occupied with planting or harvesting. Some stories are not to be told to "outsiders." Further, the stories are not only for children.

MacDonald (1993, quoted in Fixico, 2003, p. 90) describes Navajo storytelling as pedagogy for all ages of listeners:

> But the coyote stories taught to children become more complex as the years pass, providing older children with appropriate cultural guidelines. Other, more sophisticated stories, told by the elders, especially during the harsh winter months when there is less work to do, deal with ever more complex issues of mortality, ethics, history, and religion, which adults must learn and understand. (p. 90)

4. Participative: Listeners have a proactive, participative role in Native American storytelling, both in the creation and the interpretation of the meaning of the story. The wisdom of the Native American stories must be sought by the listener. The listener has an active role in filling in the blanks of the terse story. Further, the listener is proactive in deciding for themselves what the meaning of a cryptic story might be to themselves personally.

Among some tribal people, there is reluctance to write a story down. Once written, the power and authority (author-ity, or author's omniscience) of the text passes from the person who is the master teacher, to the impersonal written word. What is lost is the wisdom and judgment of the elder who had been authorized to tell the story (Illich, 1993). If a text of a story is written, some tribal people are reluctant to allow the story to be illustrated. Providing illustrations preempts the listener from participating by cocreating the images in her/his own mind.

5. Place-oriented: Place in indigenous cultures is a key concept for meaning-making. The Native American sense of place is rooted in the aliveness of the world around us. Thus place becomes almost another character in stories. This results in treating place as more significant than time to many Native Americans.

Place is more than mere geography. Place becomes imbued with the spirit of the events which happened there. This is a deeper phenomenon than geographical locations being memory-joggers, like "This is the big rock where the snake bit our great-grandfather." According to Basso (1996), among the Western Apache, the spirits of the people in the stories still dwell in the place of the story. They are available in that place to provide guidance to those seeking the meaning and wisdom of the story. The living rocks and trees of the story's place also keep alive the message to be passed on to future generations.

As Cajete puts it (Cajete in Eder, 2010, p. xii), "Yet, stories go beyond education and the recitation of words. Early indigenous stories related the experience of life lived in time and place. They were not only a description but an echo of a truth lived and remembered."

To better understand place, consider this brain-teaser: A man built a perfectly square house with 4 equal sides. Each side had a southern exposure. A bear came along. What color was the bear? (See the end of this chapter for the answer.)

6. Time-bending: One of the reasons that place is so important is related to the perceived malleability of time. Similar to current quantum concepts of time as non-linear, time is viewed as folding back upon itself and existing in simultaneously-present historical layers. Thus while the spirits of the actors in a story (and recall that these actors may include rocks, plants, etc.) are strongly tied to place, they are not so strongly tied to chronological time. In a sacred place where a story took place long ago, the spirits of that previous time and place exist in the present to provide guidance to those living in the present and seeking the wisdom held in that place (Basso, 1996).

7. Non-human-centric: Euro-Western stories do often have animal characters. However, when they do, those stories are rarely considered as serious moral lessons for adults as well as for children. Also, the animal characters in Euro-Western stories typically are not keepers of wisdom.

Summarizing the use of animals in stories in Navajo education, Fixico (2003) says that "According to native logic, Coyote, Rabbit, and other tricksters had a special role in helping to explain fate, irony, and folly in life (p. 90)."

Let us go back to the opening story of the little bird. What do you notice about this story? Consider three factors: first, the characters; second, the moral lessons; and third, the sources of power and wisdom in the stories.

First, consider the characters. Who are the characters? What sort of characters are they? They are a bird, a cow, and a cat. In indigenous stories, just as in this Euro-Western story, these "animals" would be characters in the story. However, instead of being the dupes or the victims, these animal characters would be present to impart wisdom and advise humans on the proper way to behave, both with each other and with the natural environment. In addition, most Euro-Western stories with animals as speaking characters are either children's stories or jokes, not important morality tales.

Second, consider the moral lessons offered at the end of the "Little Bird" story. Their sense of humor is one thing they would have in common with indigenous stories. However, American Indian storytellers typically would not tell you what is the "meaning" or "lesson" of the story. These lessons would be hidden in the story. To understand the lessons would require some familiarity with the cultural context, which is a lesson in itself about cultural norms and expectations.

Providing the three "lessons" at the end of the "Little Bird" story discourages the listener from proactively seeking meaning in the story. Perhaps even more importantly, providing ready-made meanings and interpretations fills in those spaces where the listener otherwise might supply their own meanings. This may discourage listeners from cocreating the story and making it their own.

Third, in the above "Little Bird" story, the bird, the cow, and the cat are portrayed as unaware characters. They are so stupid they don't even know the difference between a friend and an enemy.

If we were to take the Little Bird story and change it to be more like an indigenous story, we might get something like the following (completely fabricated by Rosile):

> A brave was hunting alone in the winter and became so cold he fell frozen to the ground. A buffalo was passing by. The brave said "Oh brother buffalo, let me kill you and use your hide to keep me warm, and your body to feed my family." The buffalo said "Why should I give my life to a fool?" Then the buffalo dropped a pile of dung directly on the brave's body. The buffalo walked away. The brave resigned himself to death. Instead, he soon discovered that the warmth of the dung brought life back to his frozen body. Alive again but delirious, he began stumbling in circles. A bird landed on his shoulder and whispered into his ear, "Follow me." The bird led the brave back to his teepee.

From the above two examples, the Little Bird story and the pseudo-indigenous Brave Hunter story, we see some of the differences between the indigenous and non-indigenous storytelling. The Brave Hunter story demonstrates:

a) the indirect approach to moral lessons through a terse, cryptic, cocreated story;

b) the characters which include both human and non-human;

c) status reversal of humans and non-humans.

In an indigenous story, the animal (and even rock and tree) characters are typically the sources of wisdom, from whom the unaware human can learn. The emphasis is on the interdependence of all life. The brave may have hunted alone for selfish reasons (he did not want to share his bounty). Perhaps, he thought he was a better hunter and could be more successful alone, thus contribute more to his tribe. Regardless, he did not hunt with his brothers, he hunted alone. He failed to understand the importance of interdependence, between himself and his tribesmen, and among all living beings and Mother Earth. This might be why the buffalo said the brave was foolish.

These differences in types of morality stories also suggest different pedagogies, different ways of presenting stories. For example, Sarris (1993) discusses how Native American Indian students in his classroom were extremely reluctant to discuss their personal experiences that paralleled a story of a student drop-out. Surely they, or someone they knew well, had been in such a situation? No one volunteered to comment. Sarris re-examined his methods and tried a different approach. He asked students to suggest the future of a hypothetical native student. The wall of silence was broken. With this different context, his students offered rich stories of teen pregnancies, absent parents, dropping out to work minimum-wage jobs, arrests, etc.

To Sarris, these stories clearly indicated that the students had personal experience with all these difficulties. However, the format of the lesson ("Tell us what you think will happen to this person") allowed for self-protection from telling one's own personal story. At the same time, a person could draw upon their personal experience to "fill in the blanks" in the projected scenario with the strength and conviction of personal experience, a position of power.

To summarize, indigenous storytelling is highly contextual to the point of being cryptic. It is terse in its contextuality, adding to its lack of transparency. These qualities allow the stories to be participatively cocreated, as the listener makes the story her/his own by filling in the blank spaces. These factors all contribute to indigenous stories fitting the model of "living stories" (Boje, 2001, 2008) rather than the traditional Euro-Western model of BME linear (and thus somewhat rigid and petrified) narratives.

We see that these indigenous methods of storytelling and pedagogy can offer a different way to understand and teach about ethics. When information is presented as a directive, a "should" as in "you should do X" it invites resistance and argument (Why should I? Did they?). When information is presented as an inquiry, we seek to know more in order to understand. If I am told "Thou shalt not hunt alone" and I am told a story about the terrible things that happened when someone hunted alone, I may spend my time figuring out how I can hunt alone yet avoid the pitfalls described in the story. If I am told instead "A hunter went out alone, and killed a deer with a knife," now I am curious to understand why, and how, and under what circumstances, and what future problems are likely to be encountered as a result of this action. I must draw my own conclusions about the most morally appropriate course of action. In short, I must think for myself, while drawing upon the wisdom of others.

Tips for Teaching Ethics Using "5 I's" of Indigenous-Inspired Storytelling Methods

(Adapted from Rosile, Pepion, Boje, & Gladstone, 2012)

To teach ethics from an indigenous perspective using storytelling, the storyteller can employ some indigenous storytelling methods to adapt their stories. These methods include:

1. **Indirect:** Present a "story-stem," or the beginning of a story, and ask participants to complete the story. What will happen to these characters next?

Example: The early bird gets the worm. This is a terse story, and its meaning for humans in a particular situation is open to interpretation,

2. **Inclusive:** Include non-human characters in the story. Even if they are not endowed with human speech, what does the plant tell us when it continues to produce fruit because of our tending of it? Many lessons about "giving back" and sustainability are available in the natural world. There is an important meta-message when we make the natural world into equally alive characters in our stories.

Example: The early bird gets the worm. This story includes two animal characters: the bird and the worm. We have no gender barriers, no indication that these characters are male or female, short or tall, young or old. This way, anyone can identify with the animal character.

3. **Incomplete:** Use terse stories and ambiguity to elicit assumptions, and to heighten awareness of taken-for-granted assumptions.

Example: The early bird gets the worm. Am I like the bird? What "worms," what payoff, do I seek? What does it mean to me to be early when I am seeking my payoff?

4. **In Context:** Explore the context of your stories. Principles of ethics endure, but contexts vary. Identify the relevant aspects of context, and allow participants to discover principles.

Example: If you're a bird, be an early bird. But if you're a worm, sleep late.

(From a poem by Shel Silverstein) Here we see different contexts for different actors, different points-of-view. What does the Thanksgiving holiday look like from the turkey's view?

5. **Inquiring:** Ask "What is the moral of this story?" rather than tell it.

Example: The early bird gets the worm; but the second mouse gets the cheese.

(Steven Wright) Wait a minute, these stories are direct opposites of each other. There are two lessons, and they contradict each other. Should I be early and be first to the goal, or should I hold back and wait? Is one "lesson" right and the other wrong? Is there a moral of the two stories combined? Now I am curious to figure out an answer for myself.

I offer a final example of how the importance of location typically is overlooked in our Euro-Western culture. Recall the riddle of the man with the house of 4 equal sides. It is difficult for many people because, like indigenous stories, it is not a linear cause-effect story. Its non-linearity appears cryptic. In addition, the riddle appears tricky, and it fools people because in our culture, we have a relatively poor sense of place, and of location, of geography, especially when compared with indigenous peoples. The (admittedly non-linear) crucial information is there in the riddle, but most people overlook it. Since all 4 walls had southern exposures, the house must have been built on the North Pole. In this context and location, the color of the bear would be white.

Search for Wisdom

— Dr. Grace Ann Rosile

1. *A small business owner sold a customer packaged food that was past its "use-by" date. After that customer leaves the store, what happens is ....*

   Instructions: Suggest at least 3 different endings for the story. For each story ending of what happens next, list as many different "moral of the story" lessons as you can find in 5 minutes.

2. *A student did not purchase the required textbook for a college class. During the coming semester, what happens is ....*

   Instructions: Suggest at least 3 different endings for the story. For each story ending of what happens next, list as many different "moral of the story" lessons as you can find in 5 minutes.

3. "Make hay while the sun shines." Instructions: Find out the true agricultural meaning behind this saying. Why is it important to make hay while the sun shines? Does this idea apply to other situations in life? In what situations might you use it?

4. "If a man speaks in the forest and there is no woman to hear him, is he still wrong?" What does this mean? What are "victimless crimes" like cheating on an exam, or personal use of illegal drugs? Are they truly crimes? Are they truly victimless?

5. This book began with Russell Means' retelling of his grandfather's story about "Looks Twice" who went hunting alone to feed his family, and

killed a deer with only his knife. Are you beginning to get some ideas of what this story was supposed to teach the young Russell Means? I am hopeful most readers will want to keep reading this book, to piece together the puzzle for themselves. However, in the way of Greg Cajete's "hints," I suggest some possible interpretations of this story at the end of this book in the "epilogue."

Grace Ann's Note

This concludes Part II. We hope you the readers now have a better understanding of how moral values and principles are conveyed through different forms of storytelling in both American Indian tribal cultures and Euro-Western cultures.

Next we delve into the details of businesses, beginning with a case example of Dardan Enterprises. Cofounder Dr. Daniel Stewart is both a successful entrepreneur and a well-published professor of business at Gonzaga University. He is that rare person who excels in both theoretical and practical aspects of business.

References

Basso, K. H. (1996). *Wisdom sits in places: Landscape and language among the Western Apache*. Albuquerque, NM: UNM Press.

Boje, D. M. (2001). *Narrative methods for organizational and communication research*. London: Sage.

Boje, D. M. (2008). *Storytelling organizations*. London: Sage.

Cajete, G. A. (2000). *Native science: Natural laws of interdependence*. Santa Fe, NM: Clear Light Publishers.

Cajete, G. A. (2010). Preface. In D. Eder (Ed.), *Life lessons through storytelling: Children's exploration of ethics*. Bloomington, IN: Indiana University Press.

Fixico, D. (2003). *The American Indian mind in a linear world: American Indian studies & traditional knowledge*. London: Routledge.

Illich, I. (1993). *In the vineyard of the text*. Chicago, IL: University of Chicago Press.

Macdonald, P., & Schwarz, T. (1993). *The Last Warrior: Peter Macdonald and the Navajo Nation* (p. 17). New York, NY: Orion Books, (cited in Fixico, 2003, p. 90).

Means, R., & Wolf, M. J. (1995). *Where white men fear to tread: The autobiography of Russell means*. New York, NY: St. Martin's Press.

Rosile, G. A., Pepion, D., Boje, D., & Gladstone, J. (2012). The Ontology of Diversity: Pedagogy for Native American Ethics and Philosophy at *Research, pedagogy and other institutional practices: An interdisciplinary conference on diversity in higher education*, conference at New Mexico State University, Las Cruces, NM (March 9, 2012).

Rosile, G. A., Pepion, D., & Gladstone, J. (2012). Daniels Principles of Business Ethics and Tribal Ethics: Using Indigenous Methods of Storytelling to Convey Moral Principles. Jan 2012 DFEI Conference Presentation, Hotel Encanto, Las Cruces, NM.

Sarris, G. (1993). *Keeping slug woman alive: a holistic approach to American Indian texts*. Berkeley, CA: University of California Press.

Part III
Trade, Barter, and Ethical Business Relationships

Ethical Business Practices in Dardan Enterprises

Daniel Stewart

Dardan Enterprises is a commercial construction firm that does business in the US Pacific Northwest. Commercial construction means that we build business structures, not residential homes. My name is Dan Stewart (Spokane Tribe) and I started Dardan in 2004 with a long-time friend of mine who had many years of construction experience. His technical skills, coupled with my business skills, made for a good match. We have shown steady growth over the years and in 2013, we were selected by the US Small Business Administration as an Emerging Leader company, which means that we were identified as one of America's most promising small businesses, poised for future growth.

It is difficult to say where the source of our business ethics lies. A conventional definition of ethics is: a system of values and beliefs that define what is right and wrong. So, in order to distinguish the source of an individual's ethics, you would need to identify the source of that person's system of values. For Dardan, we don't rely on any particular ethnic source or academic framework. The values of each founder and each employee are unique — heavily influenced by our own family background, ethnicity, spirituality, education, community, and professional training.

Ethics is What You Do

Within any organization, value systems are established and embedded over time, building from the diverse personal values held by individual employees. Thus, Dardan's organizational ethics are based on a hybrid system, influenced by the beliefs and actions of its many contributors. As an organization, we make decisions that, over time, come to define the type of company Dardan is. Every choice is a reflection, often subconscious, of what our enacted priorities are. As such, we define our values not only by what we say we believe, but by the actions we take. These values then become the source of our ethical code — right or wrong choices defined by the values we have enacted across time and across decisions.

Sustainable Business — At Dardan, our number one value is sustainability. But not the type of sustainability you might be thinking of. Usually when people think of sustainability, they think of the health of our natural ecosystem. When Dardan talks about sustainability, we talk about the health of our business. Can the business sustain itself over time? So, sustainability for us is really about generating enough profit today that we can continue to operate tomorrow.

Misconception — One common misconception about business owners is that they must be taking home a lot of money. The reality is that most of the profit in a small business goes right back into the business. In a competitive environment, a business must reinvest in itself in order to remain competitive. If it doesn't, the competition will improve faster than them and there is a risk that the company will go out of business.

Reinvestment — In other words, a business is not sustainable without continual reinvestment. For example, what if I complete a project today and, after I pay all my expenses, I still have $100 left? I could take the $100 profit and buy something nice for myself or my family and friends. We all like to buy something nice for our families and friends. However, if I do that, there is a risk.

Competition — Say my competitor also makes $100 profit today. If I take my $100 and buy something nice for others and he takes his $100 and buys a nice piece of business equipment, then I've hurt my future business. You see, the next time we both compete for a job, he will be able to do the same job better or cheaper than me because his equipment is better than mine. So, in order to remain competitive, I must constantly reinvest into the company or risk falling behind the competition. Thus, the next time you become focused on how much money a company is bringing in the door (its revenue) remember that most of the profit (revenue minus expenses) is reinvested back into the company. Most small business owners aren't taking home "all that money."

Owner's Role — If there's anything left after reinvesting in the company, then the owner gets to take a paycheck. In the early years of Dardan, there were months when the owners did not take a paycheck at all because employees and subcontractors were always paid first. I guess you could say that our values influenced the choice to create secure employment for our employees before taking care of ourselves. However, there are also times when we take home more than our employees. Some might argue that this is unfair or unethical. Why should we make more than the employees? Is this unfair exploitation of labor?

Owner's Risk — The answer is no, if you analyze the risk factors. In business we often refer to the idea of risk capital. Risk capital is money that owners put invest in the business, with the potential risk of losing it all with no return whatsoever. So, all the money I keep putting back into the business, I could have been putting into the bank, where it would have been nice and safe. By not putting it into the bank, I have risked it all in the business.

Risk for Reward — If Dardan goes bankrupt, as an owner I am the only one who loses the investment. As such, my risk is much higher than any employee. What justifies risk? Reward. If I can take home enough reward to justify the risk, then the risk is worthwhile. How much risk are we talking about? Small business owners can literally be at risk for millions of dollars at any given moment, on any given day. We have debt that we owe to banks, subcontract obligations that must be paid, liability risks, and potential monetary penalties for non-performance. In other words, owners have obligations that must be covered if catastrophe were to strike, even if it were through no fault of our own. Higher risk is only justifiable with higher reward. Trust me when I say that some days it feels as though depositing the money in the bank would be the easier way. It would be safer, for sure.

In the end, we do believe in rewarding our employees fairly and we compensate them as such. So, the ethical question that remains is not whether business owners should be rewarded (they should), but what should business owners do with their profits after fairly compensating employees, various creditors, and themselves?

As previously stated, most profit goes back into the business, but we also believe in supporting our community. By community, I don't mean the other businesses who buy our construction services. I mean we support local charitable causes whose values align with our own. Dardan has been fortunate to have a steady stream of business over the years, so we like to contribute towards worthy causes. For us, this has meant sponsoring many youth organizations.

Community Involvement — We have sponsored dozens of local youth sports organizations because we believe youth sports is an excellent way for children to learn leadership and teamwork — skills necessary for their future. We have also sponsored many local music events because we believe that music teaches self-discipline and creativity. We contribute to charity with an open heart and with no expectation of any sort of direct financial return to Dardan from the donation. We also contribute our managerial and technical talents by volunteering with local non-profit organizations as often as feasible. We contribute as an extension of our own values, sharing those values with others and helping develop those values in the greater community.

Another issue in Native American business ethics is the exploitation of our Native American heritage for profit. One strategy Native American businesses often use for marketing is the branding of a good or service as "Native American," a strategy called the culture-of-origin strategy (Stewart et al., 2015). The ethical issue here is whether individuals should make profit by exploiting a collective good.

Respect for Cultural Heritage — American Indian culture and identity do not belong to any particular person or business and, as such, one might question the rights of any individual or company to make a profit based on an ethnic identity and culture which belongs to the entire community. Dardan does not sell or market its construction services based on American Indian ethnicity. It just happens to be that there is nothing particularly "indigenous" or cultural about our service. We build to architectural specs that others have created ahead of time, so the value of our construction services isn't increased by building as a "Native American" firm. However, we support others who do follow this strategy, so long as the cultural branding is done with respect towards both the interpretation and preservation of the native culture.

Eco-Sustainability — The most prominent link between construction and American Indian culture is probably a cultural sensitivity towards environmentalism. So, what about eco-sustainability? You might have come to this chapter thinking that's what you were going to read about. I will tell you that environmental sustainability is extremely important to Dardan. Our business builds structures on my Spokane tribal ancestral grounds. As I move around town, I often look into the local hills and valleys and imagine what my Spokane ancestors would have been doing here in their time. Often, I feel the presence of their spirits. This historical attachment to the land creates in me a desire to treat the land respectfully, adopting a physician-like attitude that Dardan should, "above all, do no harm."

In order to enact this value, Dardan takes a multifaceted approach. First, we have purposely adopted a strategy that focuses primarily on improving existing buildings instead of building new ones. The majority of our business, by design, is the remodeling of existing office space for building owners and tenants who want to upgrade their current office space.

Eco-Benefits — This strategy has multiple benefits. First, it decreases the need to break ground on new structures. Second, when we remodel an office space, the new space is almost always more efficient and eco-friendly than it was before. Part of this increase in efficiency is through increasingly high standards that are part of modern building codes. Part of the increase is through improvements in technology within the newest electrical and mechanical systems that go into the remodeled spaces.

In addition, we work with our clients to encourage them to become eco-friendly. We actively encourage the use of renewable energy and green technologies when customers have those options available. We also repurpose or recycle as much material as we can from construction sites. This creates less of burden for our local landfills.

Health — More recently, we have also been encouraging our clients to design spaces that are not only friendly to the natural environment, but also support the wellness of the occupants and employees who work in the space. Thus, our definition of sustainability is expanding to include the health of people within the building.

Stakeholders — In sum, Dardan seeks to engage in ethical behavior which reflects the values and beliefs of our stakeholders. By stakeholders, I mean all those people and organizations that hold a stake, or interest, in our firm doing the right thing. Employees have an interest in stable, fair employment at a living wage. Creditors have a stake in the long-run profitability of the business so we can repay our debts. Owners have a stake in rewarding their financial risks. Buyers have a stake in receiving a quality build at a fair price. Tenants have a stake in healthy work environments. Finally, our community has a stake in ensuring Dardan maximizes the energy-efficiency of its buildings, enabling local businesses to be good stewards of the natural environment. By paying attention to the diverse needs of our stakeholders, Dardan hopes to positively impact the long-term well-being, or sustainability, of both the business and our community.

Search for Wisdom

— Dr. Grace Ann Rosile

1. Into which category would you place Dardan Enterprises: Elders, Masters, Migrators, or Traders (based on Table 5.2 in Chapter 5)? Why?

2. When evaluating an organization's ethical standards, what information can you get by what they say they believe? What information can you get by observing what they do? What can/should a person do when direct observations of a company's actions seem to contradict their stated values?

3. What actions does Dardan take to demonstrate its values and ethics in its business?

4. What values are reflected in Dardan's support of local community activities?

Grace Ann's Note

Many thanks to Dr. Dan Stewart for sharing his expertise and experience as an entrepreneur in the highly competitive world of construction! We will hear his voice again at the end of this section, with his business location decision-making exercise.

In the next chapter, we hear the personal stories of how tribal values were taught to Dr. Verbos, Dr. Kennedy, and Carma M. Claw. These three tribal women are now faculty members in colleges of business. These authors discuss how tribal values translate into leadership behaviors in the business world. They also provide us with rich case examples of tribal businesses explicitly bringing American Indian values into the running of those successful businesses.

Reference

Stewart, D., Gladstone, J. S., Verbos, A. K., Katragadda, M. S. (2015). Native American cultural capital and business strategy: The culture-of-origin effect. *American Indian Culture and Research Journal, 38*(4), 127–138.

Native American Values Applied to Leadership and Business Ethics Education

Amy Klemm Verbos, Deanna M. Kennedy and Carma M. Claw

Introduction

Boozhoo (Greetings)! Amy Klemm Verbos is an enrolled citizen of the Pokagon Band of Potawatomi, which is centered in Dowagiac, Michigan. Deanna M. Kennedy is an enrolled member of the Cherokee Nation of Oklahoma. Carma M. Claw is from Utah, where she is an enrolled member of the Diné Nation (also known as the Navajo Nation). We are sharing with you a sense of our tribes' ethical values and how they may be applied to business and leadership, the implications for business ethics education, and the implications for business practice, which we believe are profound and could be a part of a new era for business. In this chapter, we focus on Potawatomi, Cherokee, and Diné values. We note that these values may be similar to or somewhat different than the values of other Native American tribes. There is great diversity in

111

Indian Country. The Bureau of Indian Affairs recognizes government to government relationships with 567 tribes, and within these diverse cultures, many distinctions and differences in values may occur. We are not well versed in all tribes' values and ethics, and this is a boundary condition of this chapter.

Another condition of this chapter is that we do not convey these values in a traditional legend story form. We do not believe that the legend stories are ours to tell in writing, especially outside of their cultural context. Rather, we endeavor to give a sense of the underlying ethical values as we understand them and provide our interpretation of how they apply to business ethics education and practice. The interpretation of these values does differ across cultural contexts but it is our hope that the spirit of what was meant by the values to our ancestors and the benefits that they may bring to succeeding generations are what you will glean from this chapter.

Seven Grandfather Teachings

The Seven Grandfather Teachings originate in an oral sacred story, passed down over millennia by the Potawatomi and Ojibway, that tells of human responsibilities given by spiritual beings to the first elder as gifts.[1] These gifts translate into English as: wisdom, bravery, respect, honesty, love, humility, and truth. The meanings are in some ways different from western notions, but each is readily recognizable across cultures as virtuous. However, one significant difference from Western notions is that the values are *human responsibilities*. Moreover, the teachings are interrelated and interdependent. If you do not do one, you are doing its opposite — a negative or evil (e.g., hate or indifference, opposite of love, is evil and wrong). *Wisdom* comes from experience and is to be used for the people. *Bravery* is to persevere in difficult times and act

---

1. One telling of this story by an Ojibway author is found in Benton-Banai (2010). This is not the only telling of this story that is informed in this chapter. However, indicating that there is "author unknown" belies the many people who have passed this story down over time.

courageously. *Honesty* is to act with good intentions, genuinely, without fraud or deception. *Love* is to care for and be generous to others, including future generations. *Respect* is to honor all of creation, not just other people. *Humility* is to remember that one is not greater or lesser than any other. *Truth* is to have integrity in all dealings and to speak the truth. Reflecting on the Seven Grandfather Teachings, it is clear that it is difficult to follow all of the teachings at all times. Yet that is what we are to do in all of our behaviors — in our personal lives as well as in doing business with others.

Cherokee Nation under Chad "Corntassel" Smith

The Cherokee Nation is one of the largest American Indian Tribes in the United States with over 300,000 members. Since the relocation of the Cherokee in the 1830s to Oklahoma, the Cherokee people have struggled with social and economic hardship. Moreover, questionable business and government practices have created internal and external adversity to establishing, developing, and sustaining prosperity for members. As such, it is a noted accomplishment of recent leadership to provide the Cherokee Nation with the ethical leadership needed to overcome the past mismanagement of tribal affairs. Chad "Corntassel" Smith served as Principal Chief from 1999–2011. Under his leadership the Cherokee Nation made advancements in social and economic areas, improving the educational, language, and cultural programs as well as increasing assets, profits, and jobs. In his book presenting leadership lessons, Chief Smith tells stories of his experience and the way 12 cultural values representing the Cherokee way of life are reflected in his decisions and behavior (Smith, 2013). These values include respect and acknowledgment, determination and persistence, integrity, leadership, communication, confidence, cooperation, responsibility, teaching, patience, humility, and strength.

The 12 Cherokee Values presented by Smith (2013) are defined as follows. *Respect and acknowledgment* is to hold each other sacred.

Determination and persistence is to keep at it and refuse to give up. *Integrity* is to do the right thing and complete the task, whether or not anyone is watching. *Leadership* is to lead by example, the way we want to be treated and the way we want others to act. *Communication* is to interact and communicate with others. *Confidence* is to be sure of yourself and your abilities, but also be humble. *Cooperation* is to help out one another. *Responsibility* is to be committed to the task or assignment given. *Teaching* is to share knowledge and wisdom so that others may learn. *Patience* is to be patient in all situations. *Humility* is to never think you are better than others. *Strength* is to be strong in all tasks you perform and remember the strength in the Creator and the ancestors that came before you. It is evident that these values are similar in many respects to the Seven Grandfather values.

To demonstrate the way these values give leadership perspective Chief Smith conveys the following story about a Goodwill Store employee. An abridged version of the story appears below (Smith, 2013, p. 38):

> When we feel "down" or when we ask ourselves if our work is valuable or appreciated, we should remember the inspiration from the trials and tribulations memorialized in our history.
>
> In addition to historical inspiration from our ancestors, I remember once, about a decade ago, dropping items off at a Goodwill store. An old man sat in a lumpy, beaten-up sofa situated in a semi-trailer. He looked through the discarded items, sorted them, and gave receipts. At first glance, I thought, "What a boring job," but then immediately it hit me that I would give my arm if my deceased father could be there doing that work. It would have been work enjoyed and work done well. It would have been work that ultimately helped poor people by making furniture and clothing available. I immediately felt bad for thinking the job was undeserving or without value.

This story invokes a number of the Cherokee values. The interaction with the Goodwill employee conveys a sense of respect and acknowledgment about the employee's task, humility in considering the task's importance, and leadership in regarding the employee as a valued contributor to people's well-being. Additionally, the story itself represents the values of communication through the sharing of a cherished experience, and teaching, by using the story to convey a lesson about leadership. It is through living the Cherokee values at every turn and through every experience that the Cherokee Nation has sustained their fortitude and survival (Strickland & Strickland, 1991). Finally, while these values have had direct influence on the economic success of the Cherokee Nation, they are meant for a more basic purpose, to ensure "a happy and healthy people" (Smith, 2013, p. 35).

Sa'ah Naagháí Bik'eh Hózhoon

In Diné (Navajo) culture, the overarching concept of Sa'ah Naagháí Bik'eh Hózhoon is the fundamental principle used to inform The People (Diné means "The People" in the Navajo language) of how to live ethically. A loose translation of the term is "one's journey of striving to live a long, harmonious life" (http://www.uapress. arizona.edu/Books/bid2464.htm). Long is often defined as 102 years through traditional stories, and harmonious is often tied to understanding one's place as a human in the universe. The virtues offered by the seven Grandfather Teachings and the twelve Cherokee Values are also embodied in this concept, as are many others. Hence, we use this concept to offer an interpretation of the Diné's cultural process of instilling values to foster ethical behavior. In Diné, everything (and everyone) has masculine and feminine qualities and each quality is desired to maintain balance. Consequently, the Sa'ah Naagháí portion is considered the masculine part and Bik'eh Hózhoon is considered the feminine part.

Sa'ah Naaghíi Bik'eh Hózhoon is the educational philosophy and principle framework used by Diné College, which is located on the Navajo Nation (http://www.dinecollege.edu/about/philosophy.php).

While Sa'ah Naaghíi Bik'eh Hózhoon was not always compart-mentalized, explained, or taught in a framework method, today Diné College identifies these as four elements: (1) Nitsahakees (Thinking), (2) Nahata (Planning), (3) Iina (Living), and (4) Siih Hasin (Assurance). The number four is a consistent reference in Diné thought and life (as in many other Native traditions), and the following are just a few examples: the four primary directions (East, South, West, North), the first four clans of the tribe, the four sacred colors, the four seasons, and the four sacred mountains. This section discusses only the Nitsahakees (Thinking) segment of this concept as applied to instilling values.

In the Nitsahakees (Thinking) segment, "thinking" includes conscious, constructive contemplation to become self-aware (i.e., understanding your autonomy as well as your relationship to everything around you). Along with other developmental learning, one of the earliest instructions for a Diné child is to learn to introduce themselves using the Diné clan system. This one small instruction is a paramount step in educating young individuals because it is a part of the necessary foundation to orient oneself in relation to family, community, nature, and the universe. The clan system allows a person to assert being Diné by beginning all interactions with others through acknowledg-ment of their four clans, including mother, father, maternal grandfather, and paternal grandfather, respectively. Even before a child learns to speak, parents will tell the child "because this person is your mother's clan, you can address them as mother" (replace each instance of mother with any other relationship and the same applies).

In Carma's interpretation, this practice of "thinking" encourages deeply rooted values because it is an individual commitment based on self-identity, self-awareness, and self-discipline. All of these aspects will develop, change, and adapt through lifelong education, and through the practice of this framework. Self-identity encompasses knowing your history (where you come from — beginning with the clan system) and in maturity, thoroughly understanding your individual values and beliefs; self-awareness as stated above includes understanding your place in all relationships, as well as your current position in relation to your stance on values and beliefs (e.g., do your actions and behaviors truly match your identified values and beliefs?), and self-discipline involves taking the necessary actions to align your behavior with your values and beliefs (are you honest with yourself to make changes?).

Aronilth's (1992) "Foundation of Navajo Culture" explains that one owes it to himself or herself to know who he or she is at his or her core; each person has his or her own path and pace for understanding who he or she truly is or defines himself or herself. Knowing only comes through individual experiences and self-discipline, and true education and learning is not one that is in memory, but resonates in the essence of a person. When one understands values and beliefs, those values and beliefs imbue everything in one's lives; for example, in having respect for oneself, then one respects others; by valuing differences, one is accepting of others; and, through valuing knowledge, one seeks the wisdom of others and imparts their own.

Deep-rooted values such as autonomy (T'aa Hwo' Aji T'eego), knowledge, self-sufficiency, love, compassion, empathy, generosity, thankfulness, strength, listening, kindness, acceptance, sharing, endurance, equality, uniqueness, individuality, balance, harmony, kinship, justice, and others are instilled by family, extended family, community, and through stories, legends, and ceremonies of ancestors. This basic, but imperative, foundation of self-identity is established to allow focus on developing and instilling values instead of being confused by a lack of foundation — "Who Am I?"

The Sa'ah Naaghíi Bik'eh Hózhoon concept is a continuous, repetitive process to strive for balance within each component. Additionally, the framework allows and encourages development beyond the individual to account for interactions with family, community, nature, and the universe. In summary, Sa'ah Naaghíi Bik'eh Hózhoon is a very distinctive and evolutionary process that develops and adapts throughout one's life, and is therefore, a very personal, individual, and unique experience for each person.

CASE EXAMPLE

Sacred Wind Communications

Established in 2004, Sacred Wind Communications is a privately owned telephone and Internet service provider located on the Navajo (Diné) Nation in New Mexico. The company serves residential, business, and government customers both on and off the Navajo reservation. To most non-Diné, the company website would appear to be a standard business website; however, the image and colors of the company logo, location of company headquarters, and company name are very different from most companies. Moreover, Sacred Wind Communications explicitly incorporates Diné values into its business practice as shown by the excerpt from the website, "The Winds are the underlying force that unifies everything and provides the means of communication between all elements of the natural world" (http://sacredwindcommunications.com/Sacred_Wind_Communications.aspx). In a culture where the acceptance of a new technology can sometimes be difficult, this particular statement seems to indicate that the company may understand how to address concerns about the impact of technology; that is, to bring the importance of technological advancements into the culture in a culturally appropriate manner. The underlying Diné values are further represented in business operations through efforts in various community outreach programs during its first decade of operations. Programs such as adult computer training and education (to use newly available services), college scholarship funds, toy drives for children, food drives, youth sports sponsorships, and establishing "a nonprofit affiliate, Sacred Wind Communications Community Connect" (http://www.sacredwindcommunications.com/Community_and_Links.aspx) are just a few examples of its dedication to lifelong learning and education, to children and youth, and to community, all values of the Diné.

Implications for Business Ethics Education

The human responsibilities found in the Seven Grandfather Teachings provide an ethical framework for values-based business practices and decision making. When taking an action or making a decision, it is just a simple step to consider — is this in accord with the Seven Grandfather Teachings or am I enacting an opposite of one or more of the Teachings? Verbos and Humphries (2014) have provided a few ways that these Teachings may be brought into management classrooms, through analysis of CEO behaviors, self-defined team charters that enact these values, and discussion starters. We will not reiterate the specific exercises, but encourage you to read about them and extend them by incorporating the Seven Grandfather Teachings into analyses of current events or ethical decision scenarios.

The 12 values of the Cherokee Nation are part and parcel of ethical business practices; and the stories by Chief Smith showcase a relevant approach for business ethics education. That is, an effective way to teach these lessons is through telling stories. The business stories we have shared demonstrate the way cultural values provide perspectives to situations in which leaders can make decisions, take actions, and influence outcomes. Indeed, Verbos, Kennedy, and Gladstone (2011) specifically discuss the way stories may enrich learning and create self-discovery in management education. Thus, stories of Native American values may bridge conversations about business ethics and leadership behaviors in diverse contexts.

The Sa'ah Naaghíi Bik'eh Hózhoon concept is a persistent, repetitive, and adaptive process striving for stability, continuity, and longevity. Business students could follow this same process to instill ethical thought and decisions. The framework would allow them to participate in the multifaceted, conscious assessment to orient themselves within business and community within which it operates. What values and principles do they pride themselves on? What role and place do they have in relation to family, community, nature, and the universe? A key factor in applying this concept to business education is longevity; for some reason the value of longevity seems atypical in today's enterprises where quarterly, semi-annual, and annual profits are supreme. Another key factor is harmony; again, it seems that most companies are often highly profit-driven without adequate or balanced consideration for its employees, community, nature, or the universe.

Implications for Business

Throughout Indian Country, tribal enterprises are springing up that are increasing the functional capacity of communities. These enterprises create jobs for people who have been discriminated against in the dominant culture, expand local economies, and provide dividends to the tribe that may be used for social services or be paid to tribal members. One excellent example of what can happen with this type of tribal enterprise model is Ho Chunk, Inc., a twenty-year-old holding company incorporated by the Winnebago Tribe of Nebraska that is run by an executive team that is 100 percent Native American and is headed by its CEO Lance Morgan (http://www.hochunkinc.com/). This holding company owns more than 30 businesses employing more than 1000 people organized into four divisions: Construction Services, Professional Services, Business Products, and Consumer Products (http://www.hochunkinc.com/). The diverse industries in which it operates include "information technology, construction, government contracting, professional services, wholesale distribution, office products and technology, logistics, marketing, media and retail" (http://www.hochunkinc.com/today.html). Ho Chunk, Inc. demonstrates its commitment to the people of Winnebago, Nebraska, through its involvement in a down payment assistance program for new homeowners (http://www.hochunkinc.com/housing.html). It also provides pre-owned vehicles to the community on fair terms through its Rez Cars subsidiary (http://rezcars.com/). These activities help to make housing and cars more available to the people of the Winnebago Tribe of Nebraska.

Beyond tribal communities, ethical frameworks such as the Seven Grandfather Teachings, Cherokee values, and Sa'ah Naaghíí Bik'eh Hózhoon could make a substantive contribution to resolving some intractable social problems. As an example, there would be no question that employees must be paid a living wage as it demonstrates love, respect, truth, and wisdom. If you care for another, you would want wages to cover his or her family's needs. If you respect a person and his or her work, it is only fair to pay a living wage. It is a traditional Native American value to be generous in helping others to meet their needs, thus, truth would also require living wages. Finally, wisdom would suggest that the true cost of labor be paid by the company benefiting from it rather than to require the community to make up for shortfalls in wages through social services. Moreover, under the Sa'ah Naaghíi Bik'eh Hózhoon concept, the business would acknowledge its place in the community and as a provider for its employees and understand that living wages are necessary for harmony and balance.

On the other end of the spectrum, the CEO overpayment problem would disappear under the Seven Grandfather Teachings. Humility would keep CEO pay from reaching the lofty and some would say ridiculous heights presently found in corporate America. In leading by example under Cherokee values, leaders would offer a part of their pay to lessen the inequality gap. And under the Sa'ah Naaghíi Bik'eh Hózhoon concept, the unsustainability of such practices would become evident.

While we assert that Native American values can be used as an ethical framework, these values may serve a more endearing and sustainable purpose. Indeed, Chief Smith of the Cherokee Nation explains that the Cherokee values may help you frame your social, economic, and political past but it is important to know where you are going and how to get there (Smith, 2013). Specifically, Chief Smith proposed a 100-year plan that not only considered the legacy of the people but how the cultural values would guide decisions and actions to get there. Likewise, the Sa'ah Naaghíi Bik'eh Hózhoon concept is a persistent, repetitive, and adaptive process striving for stability, continuity, and longevity. A business could identify its values and principles, orient its place in the community, nature, and the universe, and consider its sustainability from a long-term, balanced perspective at harmony with its environment. This approach of long-term planning paired with cultural values could be a driver of sustainability planning in businesses industries (see e.g., seven generation planning by the Iroquois Nations; Vecsey & Venables, 1994). Finally, because the practice is very unique and specific to the participant, the resulting plan could lead to a competitive advantage.

Conclusion

This chapter merely scratches the surface of the ways in which Native American values and ethical processes might enrich and benefit business education and business practice. Yet it contains ways in which students and business leaders may reorient their thinking to solve some of the seemingly intractable problems facing society today. Moreover, exploring these values can assist in meeting the purpose of the Principles for Responsible Management Education (PRME) found at (unprme.org) to increase the capacity of our students to become generators of sustainable value for business and society and work for a more inclusive and sustainable global economy (Rasche & Escudero, 2010; Waddock, Rasche, Werhane, & Unruh, 2010). Verbos and Humphries (2015a, 2015b) suggest that inclusion of Native American and other Indigenous world views in business ethics education is not only wise but also is an important ingredient to realizing inclusiveness as an underlying purpose of the PRME. Moreover, it is through learning about the relevance of such marginalized world views that we can begin to enable the praxis that will change the business world (Verbos & Humphries, 2015a, 2015b). We encourage greater exploration of the potential for Native American values to contribute to the betterment of our world.

Grace Ann's Note

Many thanks to Verbos, Kennedy, and Claw for sharing their illuminating personal stories, and for providing practical examples of tribal values as the bedrock of so many successful businesses!

In the next chapter, Boardman offers a long-term deeply historical overview of similarities and differences in traditional indigenous trading practices versus Euro-Western practices. These two different styles of trading came from very different sets of cultural assumptions. Boardman uncovers these assumptions to reveal the roots of conflicts arising from unmet expectations on both sides.

References

Aronilth, W. (1992). *Foundation of Navajo culture*. Tsaile, AZ: Navajo Community College Press.

Benton-Banai, E. (2010). *The Mishomisbook: The voice of the Ojibway* (2nd ed.). Minneapolis, MN: University of Minnesota Press.

Rasche, A., & Escudero, M. (2010). Leading change — The role of the principles of responsible management education. *Journal of Business and Economic Ethics, 10*(2), 244–250.

Smith, C. C. (2013). *Leadership lessons from the Cherokee nation: Lessons from all I observe*. New York, NY: McGraw Hill Education.

Strickland, R., & Strickland, W. M. (1991). Beyond the trail of tears: One hundred fifty years of Cherokee survival. In W. L. Anderson (Ed.), *Cherokee removal: Before and after* (pp. 112–138). Athens, GA: The University of Georgia Press.

Vecsey, C., & Venables, R. W. (1994). *American Indian environments: Ecological issues in Native American history*. New York, NY: Syracuse University Press.

Verbos, A. K., & Humphries, M. T. (2014). A Native American relational ethic: An Indigenous perspective on teaching human responsibility. *Journal of Business Ethics, 123*(1), 1–9. doi: 10.1007/s10551-013-1790-3

Verbos, A. K., & Humphries, M. T. (2015a). Amplifying a relational ethic: A contribution to PRME praxis. *Business and Society Review, 120*(1), 23–56.

Verbos, A. K., & Humphries, M. T. (2015b). Indigenous wisdom and the PRME: Inclusion or illusion? *Journal of Management Development, 34*(1), 90–100.

Verbos, A. K., Kennedy, D. M., & Gladstone, J. S. (2011). "Coyote was walking …": Management education in Indian time. *Journal of Management Education, 35*(1), 51–65. doi: 10.1177/1052562910384368

Waddock, S., Rasche, A., Werhane, P., & Unruh, G. (2010). The principles for responsible management education where do we go from here? In D. Fisher & D. Swanson (Eds.), *Assessing business ethics education* (pp. 13–28). Charlotte, NC: Information Age Publishing.

Early North American Trading Practice and Philosophy

Calvin M. Boardman

Let us be clear — trading has been around since life began. It occurs with humans, chimpanzees, fish, insects, and plants. It occurs when something or someone has something the other wants or needs. It may occur between the same forms of life or between different forms of life. It is as natural as being alive and is, in fact, essential for life. No living organism has a corner on or a greater claim to trading than any other organism. Science calls it symbiosis; economics calls it trade.

Each Trader Benefits — In a trade transaction, each thing or animal or person benefits in some way from the "transaction." Think of the bee in need of food and the clover in need of pollination. Think of the sea anemone in need of nutriment and the clownfish in need of protection. Think of the farmer in need of shoes and the cobbler in need of food. Think of the customer in need of a new coat and the retailer in need of money.

One may trade one item for another; we might call that barter. One may trade one item for some medium of exchange; we might call that a purchase. Taking something someone else has without giving something back is not trading because only one party benefits; we might call that theft. Trading must benefit both parties for it to be beneficial and lasting in a longer-term sense. If the trade is neither beneficial to both nor conducive to a long-term relationship for both, one of the parties will not come back to the trading table and it is usually that party who was negatively impacted by the trade.

Tribal Traders in North America — The earliest inhabitants of the North American continent were accomplished traders. By the time the first European set foot on the continent, trade centers and routes were firmly established and commercial activity was an important part of native culture. There were many flourishing trading centers in North America, some of which were, going from south to north, Tikal (or Mutul — the Mayan culture), Tula (or Tollan — the Toltec culture), Tenochtitian (the Aztec culture), Corazones (the Opata-Pima culture) — *all located in modern day Mexico*; Zuni Pueblo and Pecos Pueblo (the Puebloan culture), Skoaquik (Snaketown — the Hohokam culture), Cahokia (the Mississippian culture), Chillicothe (the Adena and Hopewell cultures), Knife-Heart River Basins in South and North Dakota (the Mandan-Hidatsa-Sahnish cultures, the latter sometimes called the Arikara), The Dalles (the Wasco-pam, Warm Springs, and Paiute cultures) — *all located in modern day United States of America*; and Mantle (the Wendat culture, sometimes called the Huron), Vancouver-Nootka (the Nuu'chah'nulth culture), and Akilineq (the Inuit culture) — *all located in modern day Canada*.

Trade Networks and Centers — These were the major centers of trade. In most cases, these centers were populated with literally thousands of people who called them home. There were countless other minor centers and crossroads of trade that, in total, created a network of roads, trails, and paths connecting these centers in a web not unlike those created as a result of a spider's handiwork.

While the archeological records are sketchy in some cases, it is clear that a few of these centers existed as far back as 3000 years ago. Not only has the archeological evidence shown that goods originating in outlying centers have been found at the opposite side of this enormous geographical region, but also that goods known to be of European origin made their way to much of the region well before the Europeans themselves showed up in those areas. The efficiency of this network was truly remarkable.

Valued Part of the Culture — There is evidence that these commercial activities were an important and revered part of early native culture as well. Festivals were often held upon the return of the trader who played an honored role. Warring tribes often declared a truce when it came time to conduct business; it was that important. In short, they were good at conducting business and business was an honorable calling.

What were the merchants and traders' motivations? Much the same as they are today — primarily to acquire a good with which to satisfy either a personal need or want or both. Of course, there were, and are, other motives as well — to gain prestige, to gain wealth (however you might want to define that), to gain inventory with which to trade for other goods, to acquire items to give to friends and family, and to transform the acquired good in some way into yet another good for use or for exchange.

False Clash of Community versus Business — Many contemporary American Indians and Indian Tribes have successful business enterprises. However, it has also been observed that there are some among them who believe that being engaged in business is not consistent with their cultural heritage and beliefs. For example, many believe succeeding in business requires a self-centered approach to enterprise and requires a focus on profiting from your trading partner. These beliefs are thought to be at odds with the use value, familial/tribal, community-centric approach to business. Furthermore, private property and wealth accumulation are often thought to be critical conceptual building blocks for the creation of a business. Here again, this belief is thought to be at odds with the communal ownership of resources, if, that is, ownership is considered necessary in the first place.

In spite of those widely held viewpoints, many contemporary tribal leaders are saying that Indian cultural philosophies are entirely consistent with those qualities needed to be successful in business. These leaders are working hard to create and expand tribal commercial activities and to provide opportunities for individual members to be entrepreneurs (Miller, 2012, p. 5). Certainly, the ancient historical record regarding trading supports these contemporary conclusions. But how did we get to the point where the culture of business was even questioned in the first place? How did the practice and philosophy toward business seem to change in the native community from where they were one or two thousand years ago?

Reasons for the Tribal versus Business Split — First, Indian country throughout the North American continent changed dramatically after the arrival of the Europeans beginning near the end of the fifteenth century AD. The population bases for the native communities throughout the continent were drastically reduced by inter-tribal war, military conquest by non-Indians and, more significantly, by disease primarily introduced by the non-Indian presence. Within a few hundred years, the numbers of native populations were a tiny fraction of their earlier strength.

Second, with decreasing population, there was an understandable decrease in commercial activity. With the disruption in traditional trade routes, there were further decreases in commercial activity. Third, climate changes in some areas caused disruptions in not only community locations and lifestyles but also on the usual trade routes and on the very items they had been trading. Fourth, family units were further broken up by slavery, dislocation, and starvation. Fifth, American tribes were loved to death by sometimes well-intentioned but badly thought out laws (e.g., the 1877 Dawes Act) which drastically reduced the land areas they had inhabited and mal-intentioned public policy to encourage Indian debt in order to foreclose on tribal lands. (See, e.g., President Thomas Jefferson's 1802 private notes which stated that the government should encourage "these (*tribes*) and especially their leading men, to run in debt for these (*necessaries and comforts*) beyond their individual means of paying; and whenever in that situation, they will always cede lands to rid themselves of debt"; Miller, 2006, p. 87.)

Business a Bad Word? — In short, everyday life as they had known it for millennia was changing in earth shattering ways. It is understandable that those events would have had significant impacts on the *practice* of trade but why did these events have an impact on the *philosophical beliefs* regarding commercial activity? How did profit become synonymous with greed? How did business become a bad word? This chapter suggests one way — having two business cultures come into conflict.

The story starts just over five hundred years ago, when the first European of the modern era arrived in the Western Hemisphere. Even though the Vikings arrived five hundred years prior to that, their impact did not last long beyond their landing. That was not the case for the Europeans who arrived near the end of the fifteenth century; the impact of their landing persists to this day.

Columbus — Trading began almost immediately after Christopher Columbus landed on October 12, 1492, first on Guanahani, as the natives called it (now a part of the Bahamas), then on Cuba and finally on an island he called Hispaniola (now shared by Haiti and the Dominican Republic) on December 5, 1492. His diary is replete with examples of trading activity between his sailors and the natives of the island.

Immediately, differences in trading values began to surface. On December 17, he occasioned that a few glass beads he had on board would be traded for gold that the natives had. Both parties seemed pleased with the transaction although it is likely that Columbus thought he got the better of the deal. Why was that the case? Because the differences in the things they valued allowed each of them to give up something of the same or lessor value for something they determined to be of greater value. Initially, Columbus instructed his crew not to take advantage of the natives, particularly when he found out they had gold, but those instructions were not long to last (Boardman, Sandomir, & Sondak, 2013, pp. 22–29).

Differences in Values

This discussion will focus on personal values that may have existed five hundred years ago for two sets of peoples — the native or indigenous population of the North American continent on the one hand (I) and the Euro-Western who sought to conquer, convert, and commercialize on the other hand (E). Generalizations will be expressed for both sets of people but it is a certainty that not all the people who were in a particular set would have acted and reacted like everyone else in that same set. Value diversity would certainly have existed not only between sets but also within sets. However, these generalizations may be helpful in understanding why the philosophy towards trading and business in general might have changed for the native peoples of North America over the last five hundred years.

There are six dimensions along which there was the sharpest contrast in values. In Table 11.1, each of the dimensions is numbered and has two categories: either Indigenous (I) or Euro-

Table 11.1: Differences in Values between Indigenous and Euro-Western Cultures.

Indigenous	Euro-Western
1. Focus on strong Family and Tribal Ties	Focus on Self and Individualism
2. Focus on Use Goods	Focus on Use Goods and Exchange Goods
3. Personal Property Individually Used and Owned, but Not Land	Personal Property Individually Used and Owned, including Land
4. Gift-Giving Important for Life and Commerce	Grease the Wheel, or Give Incentives or Bribes, Important for Commerce
5. Barter and Medium of Exchange Integral to Transactions	Medium of Exchange Integral to Transactions as a Store of Wealth
6. Honesty, Openness, and Fairness	Withholding Information or Stretching the Truth or Cheating

Western (E). Table 11.1 provides an overview of these dimensions of value differences. Following the table, each dimension is discussed below.

1) **I: Strong family and tribal ties.** Indian people had strong ties to their family heritage, lineage, and other members of the tribe and were socially tight as a group. Consensus, togetherness, and a dedication to the tribe were very important. The family unit was paramount and their spiritual beliefs tended to tolerate differences of opinion so long as no one was hurt (Richter, 2001, pp. 84−85). The culture encouraged persons to be generous and give of themselves and their possessions, particularly to other members of their family and tribe. And, they should do this expecting nothing in return (Vibert, 1997, p. 146). Beyond their inner circle, "Indians extended the social logic we apply to immediate family to a wider array of social relationships. For them social relationships ideally determined the form of economic relationships. A person shared freely with kinspeople without immediate expectation of return. A person shared with friends or fellow villagers in the expectation that they would eventually reciprocate" (Ballentine & Ballentine, 2001, pp. 232−233). Reciprocity was very important.

E: Focus on self and individualism. Europeans often displayed self-interested behavior, particularly economic behavior. Adam Smith, in his 1776 *Wealth of Nations*, reflected a common belief that individuals seeking their own advantage first and foremost will benefit society at large without intending to do so. In fact, individuals should seek out their own desires instead of society's desires in the process of making economic decisions (Boardman et al., 2013, p. 124). Richter described Western European capitalism during its expansion into North America as "acquisitive, individualistic, profit-seeking" values emphasizing "possession and accumulation." He noted that such European behavior would face "social disapproval (*from the Indians*) rooted in almost universal Native attitudes toward property rights, which emphasized need and use rather than possession and accumulation" (Richter, 2001, pp. 51–52). In addition, European Christian thought was exclusivist in that one could only find salvation by joining a particular church; everyone else was on the outside. Lastly, family, as a social unit, was not that important in determining one's self-identity; this was established by individual effort (Fukuyama, 1995, pp. 286–287; Richter, 2001, pp. 84–85).

Fukuyama noted that societies with high levels of familial and social identification trusted one another more than individuals within societies lacking in that same identification. High levels of trust led to commercial transactions where the possibility of fraud or mischief was practically non-existent; in other words, they could let down their guard and trust their trading partner. They also were more likely to give other members of their group preferential treatment in commercial transactions (Fukuyama, 1995, pp. 286–287). Perhaps, then, we might have expected to see more trust within Indian society than within sixteenth century European society.

2) **I: Focus on use goods.** Providing and acquiring use goods were important goals of Indian life. Wealth accumulation was not a goal in itself nor was making money from any of the transactions. If accumulation were experienced, it would likely be used for gift items or to barter in trade for something else of use. Money, currency, or media of exchange were only useful in so far as they facilitated the acquisition of items that could be used. Gifting was common (even expected) prior to any trade or was an expression of respect to one's community, that is, the person with the greatest wealth (in terms of respect and prestige) is the person who gives it away. Wealth in terms of personal possessions was not a widely held value (Ballentine & Ballentine, 2001, p. 230; Jennings, 1993, pp. 183–184; Vibert, 1997, pp. 142 and 226).

E: Focus on both use goods and exchange goods. Besides providing and acquiring goods for use, Europeans embraced the idea that we should accumulate use goods beyond our ability to use them in order to increase personal wealth and/or to make money. An increase in wealth would lead to an increase in prestige and power and, in turn, respect from other members of the community. The word *primitive*, a derogative word often used by early Europeans to describe the Indian, reflected the European bias against anyone who did not share their love of things beyond that they could use and their desire to accumulate wealth (Jennings, 1993, pp. 64–65).

3) **I: Personal property individually used and owned, but not land.** John Wesley Powell living with the Utes more than 130 years ago observed, "The greater part of the Indians' property is held in common … They own but little property at best, and the Indian has no word signifying rich or poor in its ordinary sense — that is having much or little property, but when an Indian says, 'I am rich,' he means, 'I have many friends,' or 'I am poor; I have but few'" (Wroth, 2000, p. 67). That was actually a very common European viewpoint; however, except for land, this was just not the case. Indian personal possessions were their own to use, accumulate or give away. "… perhaps the actual purpose (*of encouraging the viewpoint expressed by Powell*) was to discount and intentionally ignore Indian property concepts to better justify taking those rights and assets" (Miller, 2012, p. 12).

About 1885, Crowfood, Chief of the Blackfeet, said to the Euro/American that you cannot count land as one of your possessions. "Our land is more valuable than your money. It will last forever. It will not even perish by the flames of fire. As long as the sun shines and the waters flow, this land will be here to give life to men and animals. It was put here for us by the Great Spirit and we cannot sell it because it does not belong to us" (Crowfood, 1885). While the land was not owned in the traditional, contemporary sense, it was still considered tribal property so long as the tribe occupied and cultivated it. That philosophy in turn extended from tribal lands to individual members of the tribe. Even nomadic tribes returned year after year to the same areas determined by the seasons. While it was not owned, it was theirs.

E: Personal property individually used and owned, including land. In contrast to this philosophy, Europeans believed that things, including land, could be individually owned. John Locke, writing "Of Property" in *The Second Treatise of Civil Government* published in 1690, said an individual could take and own private property if he claimed the unclaimed and improved it in some way — in other words, worked the land. It was his labor that gave value to the land and thus legitimized the claim that the land was his (Boardman et al., 2013, p. 45). A title would be issued that reflected this ownership and, as a result, land could be bought, used, and sold. It was this belief in individual ownership that partially motivated the ill-fated Dawes Act of 1887, encouraging private Indian ownership of tribal lands and, subsequently, the selling of such lands to others, primarily the Euro/American.

4) **I: Gift-giving important for life and commerce.** As has been mentioned, gift-giving was an important and integral part of native life. It was a way to garner prestige among one's fellow tribal members, as a way to strengthen family relationships and as a way to foster friendships. It was also a common practice for initiating a trade with that person and to demonstrate that they could be trusted in the course of the ensuing trade transaction (Vibert, 1997, pp. 11, 145, 147, and 157). The American explorer Josiah Gregg noted in his 1844 journal, "As an earnest of our friendly disposition, we then produced some scarlet cloth, with a small quantity of vermilion, tobacco, beads, etc., which being distributed them, they soon settled down into a state of placidness and contentment. ... 'We are rejoiced,' at last said the elder chief with a ceremonious air, '... We will notify our old and young men — our boys and our maidens — our women and children, — that they may come to trade with you'" (Gregg, 1844/1954, p. 247).

E: Grease the wheel or bribes important for commerce. A bribe may look like a gift in that the object of both was to foster a long-term relationship but a gift typically was extended without the expectation of reciprocation. A bribe was just the opposite although, to be clear, there wasn't a whole lot of difference in substance between the two. "'Uncle John Smith,' an American squaw-man who exercised a great deal of influence over the Cheyennes, was one of the most notorious of the Mexicans' tormentors. Smith forced all traders coming to 'his Indian village' to pay tribute to him before they were allowed to barter. There was a time when they refused and he dumped their trade goods on the ground and invited all the Indians to help themselves. That was the last time they refused to pay a bribe to Uncle John Smith" (Kenner, 1969, pp. 90–91). This clearly was different in intent than the Indian approach but the result was the same — the trade commenced.

In the days of Comanche Chief Quanah Parker, "... bribes were being paid all around. This was the world in which Quanah was learning to operate: it was his introduction to how business was done in the rawboned American West of the latter nineteenth century, where corners were routinely cut and where conflicts of interest were the rule rather than the exception. Such behavior often resulted in the Indians being cheated or defrauded" (Gwynne, 2010, p. 299).

From the perspective of the Euro/American trader, a gift request from an Indian trader may have felt like a bribe as well. "In the fur-trade era, at Fort Nez Perces, too, there is ample evidence that demands that a trader like Simon McGilliveray (around 1831-33) might view as 'extortions,' motivated entirely by greed for goods, were seen in a rather different light by the people who made the demands. That the Natives viewed the goods they received as their due is indicated by several preconditions of trade: Native refusal of anything was 'almost tantamount to a battle'; trade never got under way until the Native people 'have had all from us' in the way of gratuities; and in general, 'Indians in this quarter, will help themselves to anything belonging to the Whites, without restitution.' McGillivray offered no explicit explanation for such conduct, apart from acknowledging that gifts were the customary way to 'make friends'" (Vibert, 1997, p. 158). It is clear there was a fine line between a gift and a bribe and it is also clear that both the native and the non-native populations engaged in both.

5) **I: Barter and medium of exchange integral to transaction.** Barter has been the mechanism of trade for millennia throughout the world. Media of exchange were developed as a way to help facilitate trading activity when the number of trade goods became large. For the early Native American, these included shells, beads, stones, or some combination of those. On occasion, textiles and pottery were used as well although they are clearly use goods as well.

E: Medium of exchange integral to transaction. Barter had been the mechanism of trade for the European for many thousands of years as well. Coins had been developed two thousand years before the colonization of North America began. Paper money had been invented in China just prior to the colonization process.

The issue is not that one group used one mechanism and the other another mechanism; they both used both. Differences remained not in practice but in philosophy. "At the time of the Creation, the Cherokee say, the white man was given a stone and the Indian a piece of silver. Despising the stone, the white man threw it away. Finding the silver equally worthless, the Indian discarded it. Later the white man pocketed the silver as a source of material power; the Indian revered the stone as a source of sacred power. This prophetic story underscores the profound differences in Indian and white value systems. In time, the Indian would be forced to use the white man's currency as his medium of exchange, but the white man would never appreciate the Indian's sense of the spiritual potential of an ordinary pebble" (Nabokov, 1991, pp. 32–33). That was the difference.

6) **I: Honesty and fairness.** Only first person accounts of behavior are recounted to underscore how personality differences may have played an important role in understanding why the native philosophy towards trade and business has changed over the centuries. A few of the first-hand accounts of Indian behavior, in chronological order are:

Cabeza de Vaca, a Spanish explorer who lived with the Karankawa Indians (along the coast of contemporary Texas) in the early part of the sixteenth century, quoted an Indian friend of his in 1536 that, "We (*the Karankawa*) had come from the sunrise, they (*the Spanish*) from the sunset; we healed the sick, they killed the (*healthy*); we came naked and barefoot, they, clothed, horsed, and lanced; we coveted nothing but gave whatever we were given, while they robbed whomsoever they found and bestowed nothing on anyone" (Ward, 1996, p. 6).

Francis Drake, during his second circumnavigation of the world, described in 1577, the Indians just north of San Francisco as a "people of a tractable, free and loving nature, without guile or treachery" (Debo, 1970, p. 32).

In a letter sent to England in 1621 aboard the ship, Fortune, the Pilgrims described Indians as "very trusty, quick of apprehension, ripe-witted, just" (Debo, 1970, p. 46).

In 1775, James Adair, an Irish native who was an historian and Indian trader, lived in South Carolina. He wrote, "Before the Indian trade was ruined by our left-handed policy, and the natives were corrupted by the liberality of our dim-sighted politicians, the Cheerake were frank, sincere, and industrious. Their towns then, abounded with hogs, poultry, and everything sufficient for the support of a reasonable life, which the traders purchased at an easy rate, to their mutual satisfaction: and as they kept them busily employed, and did not make themselves too cheap, the Indians bore them goodwill and respect — and such is the temper of all the red natives" (Adair, 1775/2005, p. 250).

After immigrating to America from Ireland in 1811, Ross Cox ultimately became a clerk in the American Fur

Company. In that capacity, he had many instances of working with the native population of the north west part of the continent. In 1831, he wrote *The Columbia River; or Scenes and Adventures during a Residence of Six Years on the Western Side of the Rocky Mountain, among Various Tribes of Indians Hitherto Unknown: Together with a Journey Across the American Continent*. In it, he documented the behavior of the Salish Flathead and Upper Kutenai noting that "Their bravery is pre-eminent; a love of truth they think necessary to a warrior's character. They are too proud to be dishonest, too candid to be cunning" (Vibert, 1997, p. 253).

Nathaniel Wyeth was born in Massachusetts in 1802. He was a successful business man having almost singlehandedly developing the ice industry in Boston before traveling across the continent to establish a fur trading company in the North West. On October 23, 1832, he entered into his journal that the Indians of the Walla Walla area "… are tolerably honest but will steal a little" (Wyeth, 1832/1997, p. 29).

Josiah Gregg was an explorer, trader, and frequent traveler on the Santa Fe Trail and the author of one of the most influential books on Indian trading ever written. In 1844, he published his book, *Commerce of the Prairies*, in which he stated that "They *(the Los Pueblos of New Mexico)* are, in short, a remarkably sober and industrious race, conspicuous for morality and honesty, and very little given to quarrelling or dissipation, except when they have had much familiar intercourse with the Hispano-Mexican population" (Greg, p. 187).

The famous Austrian artist, Rudolp Friederich Kurz, came to America to paint the landscape and the Native Americans who had become of such high interest in Europe. He noted in his journal on July 12, 1848, that "On the whole, the French more than any other European nation adapt themselves most readily to the Indian customs and mode of life; their easy going temper, their courage, gallantry, and la gloire are inherent virtues of the Indian" (Kurz, 1848/1970, p. 32).

E: Stretching the truth and cheating. A reminder that these are generalizations is in order; not all Euro/Americans behaved this way. Having said that, though, the historical record is replete with first accounts of bad European/American behavior:

John Lawson, an English explorer, sailed from London in 1700, seeking adventure. He was specifically steered towards Carolina where he experienced both the colonists and local Indian tribes. He wrote of his many experiences in *A New Voyage to Carolina* in 1709. "They (*the Indians*) are really better to us than we are to them. They always give us Victuals at their Quarters, and take care we are arm'd against Hunger and Thirst. We do not so by them (generally speaking) but let them walk by our Doors Hungry, and do not often relieve them. ... We trade with them, it's true, but to what End? Not to show them the Steps of Virtue and the Golden Rule, to do as we would be done by. No, we have furnished them with the Vice of Drunkenness, which is the open Road to all others, and daily cheat them in everything we sell, and esteem it a Gift of Christianity not to sell to them so cheap as we do to the Christians, as we call ourselves" (Lawson, 1709, pp. 236–236). Ironically, he met his end when he was killed by Tuscarora Indians in 1711.

William Burnet, Esq. was the colonial governor for both New Jersey and New York during the 1720–1728 time period. The following passage was taken from folder #3 of his papers from that time period: "They (*the Indians*) say also that the (*English*) traders who come in their country do cheat them very much in the sale of rum, instead of which they sell them water, which in a day or two stinks and is noisome. His Excell. told them that he was sorry that the traders have cheated them in rum, he intends to send a man that shall be no trader, to prevent their being imposed on or cheated for the future" (Burnet, ca. 1723). As a result of this promise and to encourage the Indians to trade directly with the local people, he proposed and the New York Colonial Assembly passed on July 4, 1723, the following: "A Message from the Assembly by Mr Hendrick Hansen with the Bill Entitled, An Act for paying the charges and Expenses of Wooden Houses or Sheds Built near the City of Albany for the accommodation of ye Indian Trading at Albany and for to keep them in good Repair and Desiring the concurrence of this Board thereto" (Burnet, p. 504). This structure was intended to, and presumably did, protect the Indians from the unethical business practices of the colonial trader.

Benjamin Franklin, in writing about the motives for a plan of union for the colonies in July of 1754, noted the difficulties the colonies were having with the native population and suggested that a federal union might be more effective in preventing the injustices towards the Indian. He stated that "Many quarrels and wars have arisen between the colonies and Indian nations, through the bad conduct of traders who cheat the Indians after making them drunk, &c, to the great expense of the colonies, both in blood and treasure. Particular colonies are so interested in the trade, as not to be willing to admit such a regulation as might be best for the whole; and therefore it was thought best under a general direction" (Franklin, 1840, p. 181).

Fray Francisco Atanasio Dominguez wrote in 1776 (in his *The Missions of New Mexico*) that "Regardless of the risk, however, the New Mexicans could not resist the temptation to defraud their gullible visitors (*the Comanches*), who, 'as soon as they buy anything ... usually sell exactly what they bought; and usually they keep losing, the occasion when they gain being very rare, because our people ordinarily play infamous tricks on them'" (Kenner, 1969, p. 39).

Summary

Not all individuals within a particular tribe behaved the same way and certainly, not all tribes behaved the same way. Not all European and Euro/Americans behaved the same way either. There were the English, French, and the Spanish, along with the Portuguese and German, and each of these had their unique characteristics. Of course, within a particular European culture, there were countless individual differences. Despite these differences, still we can identify trends.

It is now easy to understand why the native philosophy that commerce was a respectable profession has changed over the centuries. In addition to the myriad reasons for changes in the practice of trade, there was an evolution of the philosophy of trade as well (Rosile & Boardman, 2011). The first three chapters of Robert J. Miller's book, *Reservation "Capitalism:" Economic Development in Indian Country*, is highly recommended for its thorough analysis of historical American Indian commerce and the influence of the Euro-American on American Indian economics.

From the pens of the individuals who experienced life hundreds of years ago, we read about Indian business culture. We also read first-hand accounts of the non-Indian approach to business. The record seems to be clear. If I were asked which model I would like to do business with, I would have absolutely no problem making up my mind. I would always choose to do business with the person who conducted himself or herself like they were doing business with their best friend. And it's clear to me which model that would fit.

Indian and non-Indian individuals, particularly business men and women, can learn a lot by studying the age-old philosophy of the early Native Americans and how that has changed over time. One can understand why the Indian response to the logistical and cultural influences from the outside was to either quickly learn the new ways of doing business and play the "game" as well or better than the non-Indian, or by doing something to get even, including going to war, or by just dropping out of sight in the process of giving up. Whichever route was taken, it is easily seen how business could become a bad word. It is also well to remember that the root cause of the philosophical outcome for the North American Indian resides with the individual and not with the system. Business has always been and always will be essential to human existence.

In conclusion, Seika Fujiwara, writing in approximately 1605, created a Japanese code of business conduct in which he said, "Trade must be beneficial for both parties. We should not make money by making our trade partner worse off. If we do not share the profit with our trade partner, we may lose business opportunities in the long run. ... What is called profit is that which accrues through right conduct. Therefore, the merchant trying to make a quick profit will get less return than the merchant trying to make a profit in the long run. ... We cannot justify cheating and looking down upon foreign trade partners by focusing on these differences and disregarding the commonalities. ... Heaven will not tolerate deception, so we should not dishonor our own manners and customs" (Boardman, et al., 2013, p. 227). Those seventeenth century oriental business philosophies reflect the seventeenth century business philosophies of the North American Indian. As you read this last paragraph, reflect with whom you would like to do business, whom you would want to emulate if and when you decide to go into business, and what business model you think will be successful for millennia to come.

Hin-mah-too-yah-lat-kekt (Nez Perce) also known as Chief Joseph, spoke these words to Congress in 1879 (Boardman et al., 2013, pp. 51–61): "What I have to say will come from my heart, and I will speak with a straight tongue. ... Our fathers gave us many laws, which they learned from their fathers. These laws were good. They told us to treat all men as they treated us; that we should never be the first to break a bargain; that it was a disgrace to tell a lie; that we should speak only the truth; that it was a shame for one man to take from another his wife, or his property without paying for it. ... If the white man wants to live in peace with the Indian, he can live in peace. There need be no trouble. Treat all men alike. Give them all the same law. Give them all an even chance to live and grow. ... Let me be a free man — free to travel, free to stop, free to work, free to trade where I choose, free to choose my own teachers, free to follow the religion of my fathers, free to think and talk and act for myself — and I will obey every law, or submit to the penalty. Whenever the white man treats the Indian as they treat each other, then we will have no more wars. … Hin-mah-too-yah-lat-kekt has spoken for his people."

Search for Wisdom

— Dr. Grace Ann Rosile

In the film Tribal Wisdom for Business Ethics, Dr. Cal Boardman presents an alternative view of the exchange process of goods and services (the ask-bid process). Boardman suggests that American Indian trading before European contact reflected how relationships were more important than "profit." He suggests something like the scenario below (For the short film, see http://business.nmsu.edu/research/programs/daniels-ethics/tribal-ethics/).

SCENARIO

I am buying my father's old car. The BlueBook value for private (non-dealership) sales is $10,000.

However, my father says "I'll sell it to you for $8000."

I say "No, Dad, the car is worth more than $10,000. You have taken great care of it, it looks like brand new, you could get $12,000 for it! And I heard that this hybrid model is going for more than the book value in the market, now that gas prices are high."

Dad says "You need your money for the new baby on the way. And besides, you will save me the headache of listing and showing it."

I say "You're retired, you need to watch your money too! I have a friend who just bought the same car, not as nice as yours, and paid $12,000. New models are back-ordered because this car is so popular now!"

We go back and forth for a while, and finally agree that I will pay him $10,000 for the car.

How do I feel about this transaction? How do I feel about my relationship with my Dad? How does he feel about his relationship with me?

Would it make a difference if I was buying the car from a best friend instead of my Dad?

Would it make a difference if I was buying the car from a stranger through an ad in the paper?

Consider the exercise described in Rosile's chapter 12 in this volume. Pat was helping Kelly walk up the hill by putting hands on Kelly's shoulder blades to help. As Kelly leans more and more on Pat, their relationship becomes one of dependency and disempowerment rather than helpfulness. In what ways, if any, might that example of disempowerment relate to the relationship dynamics of selling a car?

Grace Ann's Note

Many thanks to Dr. Cal Boardman for bringing to life hundreds of years of history to help us understand the different business cultures of indigenous and Euro-Western peoples!

In the next chapter, I discuss what happens when one culture or party to negotiation is either superior or inferior to the other. This unequal power gives rise to difficulties and conflicts in relationships and in business negotiations. More equal power relations can lead to the mutual benefit of win-win negotiations. To foster equal-power relationships, I suggest a more egalitarian model of leadership called "Ensemble Leadership Theory" (ELT).

References

Adair, J. (1775/2005). *The history of the American Indians*. Tuscaloosa, AL: The University of Alabama Press.

Ballentine, B., & Ballentine, I. (2001). *The native Americans: An illustrated history*. North Dighton, MA: JG Press.

Boardman, C. M., Sandomir, A., & Sondak, H. (2013). *Foundations of business thought*. Upper Saddle River, NJ: Pearson Publishing.

Burnet, W. (1723). His Excellency Wm, Journal of the Legislative Council of New York, July 4, 1723.

Burnet, W. (1723). Esq. Personal Papers Folder #3. Gilcrease Museum. ca.

Crowfood (1885). Chief of the Blackfeet. American Social History Project. Retrieved from http://herb.ashp.cuny.edu/items/show/1543

Debo, A. (1970). *A history of the Indians of the United States*. Norman, OK: University of Oklahoma Press.

Franklin, B. (1840). *Memoirs of Benjamin Franklin: Written by himself, and continued by his grandson and others*. Philadelphia, PA: McCarty & Davis.

Fukuyama, F. (1995). *Trust: The social virtues & the creation of prosperity*. New York, NY: The Free Press.

Gregg, J. (1844/1954). *Commerce of the prairies*. Norman, OK: University of Oklahoma Press.

Gwynne, S. C. (2010). *Empire of the Summer Moon*. New York, NY: Scribner, a Division of Simon & Schuster.

Jennings, F. (1993). *The founders of America: From the earliest migration to the present*. New York, NY: W.W. Norton & Company.

Kenner, C. L. (1969). *The Comanchero frontier: A history of new Mexican-Plains Indians relations*. Norman, OK: University of Oklahoma Press.

Kurz, R. F. (1848/1970). Journal of Rodolph Friederich Kurz. Lincoln, NE: University of Nebraska Press.

Lawson, J. (1709). A new voyage to Carolina; Containing the exact description and natural history of that country: Together with the present state thereof. And a journal of a thousand miles, Travel'd thro' several Nations of INDIANS. Giving a particular Account of their Custom, Manner, &c. London. The full text can be Retrieved from http://docsouth.unc.edu/nc/lawson/lawson.html

Miller, R. J. (2006). *Native American, discovered and conquered: Thomas Jefferson, Lewis & Clark, and manifest destiny*. Westport, CT: Praeger.

Miller, R. J. (2012). *Reservation "Capitalization": Economic development in Indian Country. Native America: Yesterday and today*. Westport, CT: Praeger.

Nabokov, P. (1991). *Native American testimony: A chronicle of Indian-white relations from prophecy to the present, 1492–1992*. London: Viking Penguin Books.

Richter, D. (2001). *Facing East from Indian country: A native history of early America*. Cambridge, MA: Harvard University Press.

Rosile, G. A., & Boardman, C. M. (2011). Antenarrative ethics of native American Indian trading. *Proceedings of the standing conference on management and organizational inquiry*.

Vibert, E. (1997). *Traders' tales: Narratives of cultural encounters in the Columbia Plateau: 1807–1846*. Norman, OK: The University of Oklahoma Press.

Ward, G. C. (1996). *The West: An illustrated history*. Boston, MA: Little, Brown and Company.

Wroth, W. (2000). *Ute Indian arts & culture: From prehistory to the new millennium*. Colorado Springs, CO: Taylor Museum of the Colorado Springs Fine Arts Center.

Wyeth (1832/1997). *Captain Nathaniel L. The Journals of Captain Nathaniel J. Wyeth's Expeditions to the Oregon Country: 1831–1836*. Fairfield, WA: Ye Galleon Press.

Power Stories and Mutually Beneficial Negotiations: Fostering Ensemble Leadership

Grace Ann Rosile

Power and leadership look a bit different in some of the more community-oriented, more egalitarian societies versus the relatively hierarchical Euro-Western orientations. We examine these power and leadership differences based on the different story plotlines they engender. The story that emerges from unequal power participants typically is a story of exploitation or benevolence.

The problem is that both of these story plotlines (exploitation or benevolence) are disempowering. It is easy to see that a powerful and exploitive negotiator will take advantage of a weaker negotiating partner. It is less obvious why the benevolent attitude is also disempowering and potentially harmful. This chapter suggests ways to avoid disempowering dynamics, and instead to participate with others in creating storylines of upsurging spirals of mutual benefit.

This perspective provides a context to understand more fully the quote by Lilla Watson cited in the Preface to this volume: "If you have come here to help me, you are wasting our time. But if you have come because your liberation is tied up with mine, then let us work together."

This approach resonates with TwoTrees' and Kolan's Chapter 17 discussion of fostering productive relationships. They recommend avoiding the futile search for equality based on sameness. Instead they look for fairness in relationships based on "aligning strengths."

The storytelling perspective in this chapter suggests that before participants can align strengths, they need a suitable antenarrative to cocreate a story which reflects those collaborative dynamics. Here, we think of the antenarrative as a structure which holds the shape of the story, as discussed below.

Antenarratives of Power — This discussion begins by considering the antenarratives and the story plotlines for various cases of unequal power. Avoiding win-lose disempowerment and creating win-win scenarios of mutual benefit requires a more egalitarian leadership model. We offer such a model in the second half of this chapter. Ensemble Leadership Theory (ELT) provides a dynamic, relational, decentered, and heterarchical approach to leadership.

Power and Equal Power Relationships

Indigenous scholars and non-indigenous scholars have traced what has happened to native peoples, and how they have been exploited over the years (see, e.g., Deloria's Trail of Broken Treaties, 1974; and Bordewich, Killing the White Man's Indian, 1996). Much of the harm that has been done has been done in the name of doing good, in the name of economic development, and other well-intentioned projects.

In Table 12.1, we consider when the attitudes of indigenous and Euro-Westerns have been exploitive, and when they have been benevolent. The second dimension of this 2×2 matrix considers whether the other is seen as superior or inferior in power. All of these combinations are likely to create problems, as we explain next.

Table 12.1: Plotlines in Trading Partners' Unequal Power Relationships.

Attitude/ Power Position	Exploitive	Benevolent
Other is INFERIOR	If I see the other as inferior, and my intent is to exploit them, I see them as **Dupes**	If I see the other as inferior, and my intent is to benefit them, I see them as **Charity Cases**
Other is SUPERIOR	If I see the other as superior, and I think their intent is to exploit, I see them as **Thieves**	If I see the other as superior, and I think their intent is to benefit me, I see them as **Benefactors**

Source: Rosile and Boardman (2011).

"Dupes" and "Charity Cases" — The desire to do good is not enough. If you are working with people, especially trying to "help" people whom you perceive to be of a different power situation than you, there are always problems. If the other is seen as inferior, and my intent is to exploit, then their role in this story is the role of "dupes" or fools. If the other is seen as inferior, and I have benevolent intentions, their role in my story is that of "charity cases." This is disempowering, and often harmful.

"Thieves" and "Benefactors" — If the other is seen as superior, and they are inclined to exploit, then they are thieves or colonialist exploiters. They are stealing our resources, our ideas, our products. If the other is seen as superior, and they are benevolent, then they are benefactors. This is another potentially disempowering relationship, as we learn to depend on the benefactors. With that dependency, we learn to be unable to survive on our own, without the benefactors. Benefactors, as often was the case with American Indians, may also be misguided. A popular phrase of some of the misguided in previous years referred to the need to "kill the Indian to save the man."

Disempowering Helpfulness — How is it that people with good intentions may end up triggering disempowering and even harmful effects for those one wants to help? One of the ways to visualize this problem in a physical way is the following exercise. It is easily performed by two people.

Try This Exercise — Assume our two people are Pat and Kelly. Pat is walking up a hill, which is a gentle slope at first, then gets steeper. Kelly is bigger and stronger than Pat, and Kelly wants to help Pat with going up the hill. Kelly offers, and Pat accepts Kelly's offer to put hands on Pat's shoulder blades for some added support. They begin the walk. Pat leans back on Kelly's hands. As the climb gets steeper, Pat leans more and more. What are the possible outcomes of this "helping" behavior?

Reactions to Help — Pat, the help-ee, could appreciate Kelly's help. Pat might tell Kelly how wonderful it is to have such help. Kelly, the helper, could get tired but continue to help, and begin to resent Pat for requesting or requiring more help than Kelly is comfortable giving. Kelly could speak up and refuse to continue to help, risking that Pat will feel let down, abandoned, or betrayed. Kelly could become over-tired and drop Pat, leaving Pat physically hurt, perhaps angry and resentful. Kelly as helper might feel guilt for literally letting down the help-ee Pat. Kelly as helper could feel taken advantage of, and feel anger and resentment.

How can we avoid such hazards of disempowering helpfulness in relationships? Primarily by avoiding unequal power situations that have so much potential for dependency-inducing and unhelpful helpfulness. This focus on the qualities of relationships, as opposed to focus on the individual, is apparent in recent literature in the fields of both leadership and ethics.

We are moving towards more and more "relational" models that focus on the group and social-level leadership and ethical relationships. When those relationships are equal-power relationships, it is easier to avoid disempowerment problems. This is not a pie-in-the-sky "Let's pretend we're all equal." Instead, this involves finding out and appreciating what value is in that other person, in that other perspective, in that other culture. This might be similar to what TwoTrees and Kolan call "aligning strengths" elsewhere in this book (Chapter 17).

Value Diversity — A first step in fostering equal power relationships might be truly appreciating differences and genuinely valuing diversity. You might have heard American Indians say "We may not be rich in dollars, but we are rich in tradition, in family, in art, in culture." Our job is to recognize that value has many different forms, not just dollars. Power is not just dollars. If we can't see that value, there is no sense pretending we can. We will just end up in, at best, more misguided and disempowering attempts at helping. This appreciation is the focus of most diversity efforts in corporations today. Such efforts seek to go beyond diversity tolerance and diversity management to a true appreciation of the value of diversity.

Voice — Each person in an equal power relationship must have a voice. If we do not have our partners in business or in society, at the table with us, with a voice at the table, we cannot establish equal-power relationships. We risk disempowering. When we attempt to speak for someone else (sometimes called "double narration") we run the risk of misinterpreting and misrepresenting the other, in addition to appropriating their voice and power for ourselves. For example, when a hospital's doctors or administrators purport to speak for patients, saying "This is what the patients want" or "This is for the good of the patient" usually it is for the speaker's own good.

Win-Lose — Overall, disempowerment is greater if we have an assumption that our relationship with others is a zero-sum game. Zero-sum games are win-lose games, rather than win-win. An example is football, where for me to gain ground the other must lose that ground. This creates competitive and disempowering relationships. If we perceive that we are in a zero-sum game, we will end up in exploitive relationships. We will be either the "winners" (oppressors) or the "losers" (victims).

Win-Win — In contrast to this zero-sum win-lose situation is the example I heard years ago from a professor of anthropology. The example was of a culture where they played a game much like football. For one side to win by gaining territory, the other side had to lose territory. However, when one side appeared to be "winning" the other side would send reinforcements. Why? Because the object of the game was not to win or lose, but rather to keep playing the game. It is difficult for Euro-Western cultures to envision a game that is competitive, but has no losers.

Euro-Western culture has the saying "It's not whether you win or lose, it's how you play the game." If we truly believed this, how might our games be different? If we truly believed this, why do we also have another popular saying: "Winning is the only thing." The point is not about being competitive or non-competitive. Indigenous cultures have plenty of competitive games. The point is to be aware of how Euro-Western cultures emphasize win-lose much more than win-win scenarios.

Equal Others — If we see the other as equal we still have some problems. If we see the other as equal and the same as us, we may still perceive a zero-sum game. We may assume we must compete even harder to win the same resources that this similar other desires for themselves.

Projections — In addition, seeing the other as equal and the same as us may be projecting our own qualities onto the other. Then we can have false expectations based on those projections. We create a false simulacra of another who is like us. When the pioneer Europeans took photos of American Indians in colonial times, they would pose those Indians they saw as powerful in the same stylized way that royalty would pose in Europe, with hands positioned a certain way, etc. (Ordahl Kupperman, 2000).

Some projected the "noble savage" onto the American Indians, while others projected the "primitive savage" onto them. Neither stereotype was accurate; both involved projections of aspects of self or of society. Those projections were preconceived expectations which covered over who those other people really were.

Non-Zero-Sum Negotiating — If we see others as equal but different from us, and we have non-zero assumptions, we open up win-win possibilities for the relationship based on value differences.

Here, those same value differences that could bring about conflict can be used constructively. For example, a company does not want to increase wages. A strong union may go on strike (potentially win-lose or sometimes lose-lose). However, the union may bargain for more vacation time instead of a wage increase. The company may be happy to grant more vacation time, because of how that fits with a work schedule, or some other reason.

Mutual Change — When we perceive the other as equal, and as simultaneously both the same and different, we have a possibility for "intra-acting" (Barad, 2007). "Intra-acting" means each party is open to being influenced by the other, in a process of mutual change. This is where we can learn from each other. From an indigenous perspective, we learn also that the other may not necessarily be human. But they have as many rights, and have a life also, even if not a human life. So when we see the other as equal and simultaneously both the same and different, then we can start to perceive these differences. In these differences, we see how we might envision our own lives differently, and our own cultures and practices from a different perspective. This is when we have the greatest potential.

Different Yet Also Same — When we see the other as equal and at the same time both the same as us and different from us, this might be seen as a paradox, as an example of complexity theory, or as quantum physics. But this is when we have the greatest possibility of cocreating non-zero-sum, win-win situations. This is when we have the greatest possibility of creating collaborative, cocreated, and mutually beneficial stories.

This different-yet-same perspective is what we are aiming for in business ethics, to avoid disempowering or colonialist exploitive attitudes. This perspective involves the business *and* others, the business *and* society, and making business more inclusive and more ethical by allowing a place for equally powerful voices at the table. This approach may not persuade those whose attitude is consciously and intentionally exploitive. Rather, it is most helpful, and most likely to be used by, those businesses whose intentions are ethical, and whose concern is for preventing unintended, exploitive, and/or disempowering consequences for their trading partners (see Table 12.2).

Mutual Benefit — When we have powerful voices all sharing a desire to discover how we can benefit each other, we have the potential for synergy. When we are open to seeing the other in all their sameness and difference, we open wider the door to finding ways we can benefit each other and create mutual benefit.

An important part of creating this kind of powerful, inclusive business environment is leadership. How do we enact leadership in a situation of equal power, especially when in the past leadership often has been defined as power-over? For this, we look to pre-Columbian, pre-Euro-Western contact with American Indians. The evidence found by archeologists in those ancient cultures provides the underlying basis for our "ELT."

Table 12.2: Plotlines with Trading Partners' Equal and Unequal Power: Getting to Community Building Upsurging Spirals.

Power/ Attitudes	Exploitive	Benevolent	Cocreated Story
Other is Inferior	Dupes	Charity Cases	Exploitation Disempowerment
Other is Superior	Thieves	Benefactors	Fear/Gratitude Disempowerment
Other is Equal and Same	Zero-Sum Competition	Zero-Sum Accommodation	Projection Simulacra
Other is Equal and Different	Zero-Sum Competition	Non-Zero-Sum Collaboration	Cross-Cultural Intra-Acting and Mutual Change
Other is Equal and Same and Different	Opportunistic Competition	Opportunistic Collaboration	Non-Zero-Sum Collaborative Upsurging Spirals

Source: Rosile and Boardman (2011).

Leadership and Heterarchical Organization

We propose a model of leadership based on indigenous stories and autoethnographies (Pepion, 1999) as well as the trajectory of recent leadership theories. These relatively recent theories are more egalitarian, less hierarchical, more inclusive, and much more dynamic and flexible than traditional command-and-control models of the individual "great man" as leader. The following summary of these leadership literatures is admittedly overly simplified. Still, we hope we provide just enough detail to offer a sense of context and framing of ELT.

We selected three general categories of the more "relational" approaches to leadership. Rosile, Boje, and Claw (2016) call this "Ensemble Leadership Theory" (ELT), as presented in Table 12.3. An ensemble performance refers to situations where no one individual is the star in a TV show or movie or staged drama, or when there are several stars at once. Classic examples of ensemble acting are the TV shows M*A*S*H, Cheers, Friends, and Seinfeld. Everyone shares the starring role. We see this in the arts quite often, but less often in discussions of business leadership.

In Table 12.3, the current trends pointing toward increasingly ensemble qualities in leadership studies begin with Dispersed leadership. Dispersed leadership is when different people having different roles, all adding up to leadership. That is a bit like Ensemble Leadership, but not the whole thing. Dispersed leadership is like each person being a puzzle piece of the leadership role. Putting the puzzle pieces together creates a complete leader.

In a subtly but importantly different approach, the Distributed leadership model says you be the leader in war, I'll be the leader in agriculture. The leadership function is distributed or rotated among several individuals. This leadership is more like passing around the leadership "hat." You be the leader now, I'll be the leader later. With both dispersed and distributed leadership, some members may still have no role at all in leadership. In addition, those to whom leadership is dispersed or distributed may be a small proportion of the membership of the group.

UNIVERSITY OF WINCHESTER
LIBRARY

While some of these dynamics appear in Ensemble Leadership, they do not go as far as the historical root examples from indigenous leadership upon which ELT is based. There is not the emphasis on the process, the indigenous value for non-hierarchical relationships, and the essentially dynamic nature of life and of leadership.

The dynamism of indigenous cultures appears clearly in indigenous languages such as the Hopi language (Whorf cited in Cordova, 2007, p. 100). These languages have many more verbs than nouns. The English language has more nouns, reflecting a more static view of the world. Further, both dispersed and distributive models still rely on leadership functions as the component parts of leadership. This piecemeal, slice-and-dice approach to leadership is in sharp contrast to the fluid morphing that appears to characterize the flexible dynamic nature of leadership in the Oxaca valley of ancient pre-European Mesoamerica (See Table 12.4).

ELT emerges from the dynamism and flexibility which anthropologists found in ancient indigenous cultures, where the social organization was heterarchy (Joyce, 2010). Heterarchy involves multiple possible hierarchical as well as less-hierarchical social structures, especially flatter non-hierarchical ones. Heterarchy is more than a group of hierarchies. Rather, it includes hierarchies as one type of social structure, while also including rhizome-like networks of flexible authority patterns.

Heterarchy was a highly successful model of governance, resulting in one case in a society without hunger. Such societies were more egalitarian than present-day organization structures. It was thought that some combinations of disease and climate change brought about the downfall of these societies. However, recent reinterpretations of archeological findings from those ancient times suggest that growing inequalities were the reason for the conflicts, strife, and ultimate decline of those ancient civilizations.

Heterarchy is a key component of ELT. Heterarchy contributes to Ensemble's dynamism and flexibility, and makes it adaptable regarding who does what. It is not like the dispersed and distributed models, which focus on the individual and the interpersonal. Instead, ELT takes a broader, community-oriented view. This view has more movement, and more potential adaptability, as with a cycle or a spiral instead of the linearity of dispersed and distributed models.

Ensemble incorporates a group or community perspective, where various incarnations of heterarchy flow fluidly from one organizational shape to another. ELT posits an organic, fluid, egalitarian shape-shifting, a fluid morphing. Gerri McCulloh (dissertation 2015) cites the work of Myra J. Hird (2009), who documents how colonies of bacteria exhibit self-organizing and purposive behavior, with no apparent hierarchy, no single "leader." If bacteria can do it, and tribes can (or could) also organize without complete dependence on current-day hierarchies, surely it could work again.

In addition to the de-emphasis on hierarchy in these ancient indigenous cultures of Mesoamerica, there were other aspects of egalitarianism. For example, there was greater gender equality, with more matriarchal cultures. There were many ancient indigenous cultures with roles fulfilled by women as elders, medicine women, and other leadership roles in their tribes. It appears it was the Euro-White expectation that only males could be leaders that pushed indigenous cultures to move away from their previously more gender-balanced leadership roles.

Some remnants of these matriarchal traditions exist today. For example, among the Pueblo tribes, only men sit on the tribal council, but women own homes, which are passed down to the youngest daughter (Gilbert and Muller, Internet source, 1999). These tribal traditions are very different ways of enacting power in communities in ways that appear more gender-balanced as well as more egalitarian.

Gender-balance in positions of power is one of three factors which contribute to ethical and equitable relations in tribal cultures. The other two are greater egalitarianism of Ensemble Leadership-like styles of leadership within heterarchical systems, and typically power-equal relationships in trading. If each or all of these three factors received greater emphasis in present-day organizations, we might have greater opportunities for collaborations and for cocreating stories of upsurging spirals of mutual benefit. In such a situation, both corporations and communities would benefit.

Table 12.3: Comparison of Dispersed, Distributed, Relational, and Ensemble Leadership Approaches.

	Dispersed	Distributed	Relational	Ensemble
1. Nature of Leadership	Entity/Category	Entity/Category	Interpersonally Conegotiated	Collectively Cocreated
2. Locus of Leadership	Within the person	Shared among individuals	Within the relationship	Within the Collective "All"
3. Unit of Analysis	Individual	Multiple individuals	Multiple individuals	The community
4. Communication Patterns	Not a focus	Between select individuals	Between individuals	All channels
5. Roles	Predefined or not relevant	Shared among certain individuals who receive leader privileges	Cocreated and negotiated	Dynamic and fluid, more egalitarian
6. Hierarchy	Everyone a leader but still identifies leadership functions	Distributes pieces of leadership but top echelons still on top	Together a leader but still identifies leadership functions	Heterarchy includes all the above and also egalitarian

7. Agency	Individual each	Can be shared and usually top down	Individual and interpersonal	Collective any and all
8. Nature of the Game	Intrapersonal	In-group and out-group zero-sum	Interpersonal	Community non-zero-sum
9. Storytelling Structure or Antenarrative	Fractal Complex Repeating Patterns	Linear Beginning-Middle-End Cause-Effect	Cyclical or spiral	Rhizomatic

Source: Table from Rosile, Boje, and Claw, in *Leadership* (2016).

Table 12.4: Traditional Leadership Theory, Indigenous Values and Practices, and ELT.

Dimension/ Viewpoint	Traditional Leadership	Indigenous Values and Practices	Ensemble Leadership
1. Roles of Humans	Humans are center	Non-human-centric	Latour's Actor Network Theory; Quasi-objects (Serres) as Centers of Networks of Power
2. Roles of Non-Humans	Non-humans are the (non-agential) setting or situation, the acted-upon	Non-humans are actors and characters in the story, and sources of wisdom	Wisdom from the natural world and voices of ancestors
3. Relationships	Based on the power to influence upwardly or downwardly among ranked humans; linear; based on common goals or outcomes	Sacred in themselves; emphasize harmony and balance with non-humans and humans; networked	Relationships are cocreated and relatively egalitarian
4. Theories	Cause-effect linearity	Non-linear	Rhizomatic
5. Dualisms	Lead/follow individual/group (Cordova)	Integrative complexity; non-dualistic	Morphing, non-binary
6. Status	Hierarchical and mostly static	Heterarchical (Mills) and Rhizomatic	Dynamic, egalitarian, heterarchical

7. Power	Power-over concept with marginal consideration of power-with (Follett)	Power-with concept is embedded in tribal cultural context	Harmony and balance
8. Processes	Seek the norm, manipulate variables	Seek the exception, observe natural world	Organic emergence
9. Antenarrative Structure	Linear, cyclical, spiral	Linear, cyclical, spiral, and Rhizomatic Assemblage	Linear, cyclical, spiral, and Rhizomatic Assemblage
10. Story Cast of Characters	Humans in defined roles and power relationships within a given BME story	Non-humans and humans in networks of non-hierarchical relationships of mutual reciprocal behaviors (Cajete, 2000)	Inclusive of non-humans and responsive to resources and situations
11. Plot Trajectories	Focused, Goal-oriented	Diffused, circular, with multiple simultaneous directions	Tamara-land with multiple and simultaneous plots

Source: Table from Rosile, Boje, and Claw, in *Leadership* (2016).

Search for Wisdom

1. If we think we need to "rescue" someone, that is a warning flag that our "help" may be disempowering. My uncle tried to break up a fight outside of his cocktail lounge in California. Both combatants turned on him and he ended up in the hospital for his efforts. Can you think of other examples where helpfulness backfired on the helper, or was disempowering to the person it was supposed to help?

2. Many years ago there was a TV commercial where the catch line was "Mother, I'd rather do it myself!" Are "helpful" parents disempowering? Are youth unappreciative and disrespectful?

3. Classic "ensemble" TV shows have been M*A*S*H, Cheers, Friends, Seinfeld, and Parks and Recreation. Can you think of others? In what ways has their ensemble format contributed to their success?

4. Have you ever observed evidence of an ensemble style of leadership in a group or organization? What was that like? What were advantages? Disadvantages?

Grace Ann's note

Part III has provided insights into traditional tribal values as they directly apply to some example American Indian businesses. Boardman demonstrated Indigenous versus Euro-Western cultural differences in expectations about how to conduct business (and life). I end this section with how Indigenous and Euro-Western differences may be overcome through equal-power win-win trading stories. Ensemble Leadership promotes win-win mutually beneficial outcomes with cocreated storytelling among trading partners. However, this is not the end of the story for business success in tribal communities. There are still dilemmas such as the one posed by Stewart and Pascal, in the next chapter. Continue your search for wisdom by deciding where you would locate this hypothetical tribal business described next.

References

Barad, K. (2007). *Meeting the universe halfway: Quantum physics and the entanglement of matter and meaning.* Durham, NC: Duke University Press.

Bordewich, F. M. (1996). *Killing the white man's Indian: Reinventing native Americans at the end of the twentieth century.* New York, NY: Anchor Books/Random House.

Cajete, G. (2000). *Native science: Natural laws of interdependence.* Santa Fe, NM: Clear Light Publishers.

Cordova, V. F. (2007). Against the singularity of the human species. In K. D. Moore, K. Peters, T. Jojola, & A. Lacy (Eds.), *How it is: The native American philosophy of V. F. Cordova.* Tucson, AZ: University of Arizona Press.

Deloria, V. (1974). *Behind the trail of broken treaties: An Indian declaration of independence.* Austin, TX: University of Texas Press.

Gilbert, R., & Muller, H. J. (1999). Retrieved from http://www.unm.edu/~hmuller/The%20Business%20of%20Culture%20at%20Acoma%20Pueblo.htm. Accessed on August 11, 2016. Apparently also available at Buller, P., & Schuler, R. (Eds.) (2000). Organizations and people (6th ed.). Cincinnati, OH: Southwestern Publishers.

Hird, M. J. (2009). *The origins of sociable life: Evolution after science.* Basingstoke, UK: Palgrave Macmillan. doi: 102057/9780230242210

Joyce, A. A. (2010). *Mixtecs, Zapotecs, and Chatinos ancient peoples of Southern Mexico.* Chichester, UK: Wiley-Blackwell.

Ordahl Kupperman, K. (2000). *Indians and English.* London: Cornell University Press.

Pepion, D. D. (1999). *Blackfeet ceremony: A qualitative study of learning.* Doctor of Education Dissertation, Montana State University, Ann Arbor, MI: UMI Dissertation Services.

Rosile, G. A., & Boardman, C. M. (2011). Antenarrative ethics of native American Indian trading. In *Proceedings of the standing conference for management and organizational inquiry*, Philadelphia, PA.

Rosile, G. A., Boje, D. M., & Claw, C. (2016). Ensemble leadership theory: Collectivist, relational, and heterarchical roots from indigenous contexts. *Leadership.* First published online on June 7, 2016. doi: 10.1177/1742715016652933.

Native American Entrepreneurship: Locating Your Business ☆

Daniel Stewart and Vincent J. Pascal

Although previously overlooked as a factor in Native American entrepreneurship, there has been a relatively large amount of attention paid to the effects of economic clustering on entrepreneurship within the general US population. The current conceptualization of economic clusters is the product of several streams of economic theory.

Clusters Defined — Clusters are described as geographic concentrations of interconnected companies and institutions in a particular field or as groups of related industries located in the same region. More specifically, the National Governors Association defines a cluster as a geographically bounded concentration of similar, related or complementary businesses, with active channels for business transactions, communications, and dialogue that share specialized infrastructure, labor markets, and services, and are faced with common opportunities and threats. Thus, clusters represent geographic concentrations of businesses that share

---

☆ Adapted from Pascal and Stewart (2015).

related production inputs, specialized labor pools, distribution and communication channels, and network associations.

The process of identifying a cluster usually begins by measuring the number of firms and employees by industrial sector using association directories and existing databases. These data are then used to assess the relative concentration of related firms in a particular location. The ratio of employment or companies in a region to the same ratio for the nation as a whole generates a *location quotient*, or LQ. A LQ greater than 1 denotes a higher-than-average concentration of related firms in an area. Thus, an economic cluster is defined according to its LQ, or the concentration of firms in each region relative to the national average. LQ is calculated according to the following formula:

$$LQ = \left(E_{i,j}/E_i\right)/\left(E_{us,j}/E_{us}\right)$$

where $E_{i,j}$ refers to region i's employment in industry j, E_i is the total employment in region i, $E_{us,j}$ is the total US employment in industry j, and E_{us} is total US employment.

Cluster Types — There are three cluster categories that account for the majority of cluster development in the United States. *Traded clusters* are those developed around traded industries. These industries are not resource dependent and typically sell products and services across regions and even across countries. They locate based upon competitive considerations and employment in these industries varies markedly by region. Traded clusters are alleged to have the greatest economic impact on regional economies because of their influence on wages in local industries. Traded industries include information technology, medical devices, and distribution services to name a few (see Table 13.1 for examples). By contrast, *local clusters* develop around local industries where employment is generally evenly distributed across all regions and is roughly proportional to the regional population. These industries provide goods and services primarily to the local market or region in which the industry is located. Examples include real estate, restaurants, and retail. Lastly, *natural endowment clusters* develop from

Table 13.1: Traded Clusters in the US Economy.

Aerospace engines	Heavy machinery
Aerospace vehicles and defense	Hospitality and tourism
Agricultural products	Information technology
Analytical instruments	Jewelry and precious metals
Apparel	Leather products
Automotive	Lighting and electrical equipment
Biopharmaceuticals	Medical devices
Building fixtures, equipment, and services	Metal manufacturing
Business services	Motor-driven products
Chemical products	Oil, gas products, and services
Communications equipment	Plastics
Construction materials	Power generation and transmission
Distribution services	Prefabricated enclosures
Education and knowledge creation	Processed food
Entertainment	Production technology
Financial services	Publishing and printing
Fishing and fishing products	Sporting, recreational, and children's
Footwear	Goods
Forest products	Textiles
Furniture	Tobacco
Heavy construction services	Transportation and logistics

industries associates with the utilization of natural resources, and consequently, employment is located primarily where the natural resources are found. Examples of natural resource industries include logging, mining, and snow skiing.

Clusters and Competitive Advantage

Clusters can lead to increased productivity in cluster firms due to better access to specialized inputs and employees. In this respect, locational advantages accrue from being in a cluster because it provides for less costly access to specialized inputs like components, machinery, business services, and skilled personnel needed to exploit market opportunities. Furthermore, the specialized inputs needed for new firm formation (e.g., capital, skilled labor, suppliers, etc.) are more easily accessed within clusters, and in doing so makes it more attractive for new firms to locate within these concentrations. Likewise, cluster firms experience increased productivity resulting from specialized access to information (about the market) and technical expertise available to cluster members. This specialized access is the consequence of colocating with suppliers and other technological resources located within the cluster, which in turn facilitates communication flows.

Cluster development has also been associated with higher levels of innovation. Innovation results because firms within a cluster are better able to more clearly and rapidly perceive new buyer needs as well as new technological, operating, and/or delivery possibilities than those outside clusters. As such, clusters stimulate innovation activity. Clusters, because of their social network relationships, provide a locus for innovation activity, especially for high technology sectors. In clusters, the relationships that exist between customer and supplier industries and the organizations that support them create synergies that result in more innovation. These innovations then lead to enhanced cluster competitive positions and the strengthening of local economies. A firm is more likely to innovate if located in a region where the presence of other firms in its own industry is strong.

Clusters and Native American Entrepreneurship

Economic clusters provide advantages to cluster firms due to their proximity and access to the inputs needed for opportunity exploitation (e.g., capital, skilled labor, suppliers, etc.). Consequently, cluster development creates a competitive environment in which the barriers to entry and success are lower for the would-be entrepreneur. However, a significant proportion of Native Americans live on tribal reservations located in rural areas, often some distance from the urban centers typically associated with cluster economies. As a result, it may be difficult for many Native American entrepreneurs to avail themselves of the advantages associated with economic clusters. Still, many Native Americans live off of their tribal reservations and some federally recognized reservations are located in or near urban areas which have economic clusters. Pascal and Stewart found that Native American firms located proximate to *traded* clusters performed better that those which were not (Pascal & Stewart, 2008). Native American entrepreneurs who are located proximate to cluster economies enjoy the same competitive advantages as afforded to other firms located proximate to clusters and, thus, should be competitively advantaged compared to their Native American counterparts that are more rural and reservation-based. As such, the unique challenges faced by Native American entrepreneurs may be somewhat mitigated by the comparative advantages afforded by being located near economic clusters.

Perhaps because cluster economies provide firms with advantages that are not accorded to firms outside these economies, more new firms are created within clusters than outside of clusters. One factor that motivates firm creation is the accessibility of skilled labor needed to exploit business opportunities. Skilled labor is more readily attracted to cluster economies due to the perceived heightened prospects for employment within cluster locations and, consequently, labor is more readily available to cluster firms. Because many American Indian reservations are located in rural areas, access to specialized labor might be hindered due to geographic constraints.

Tribal Gaming and Native American Entrepreneurship

Since the early 1990s casino gaming has been a dominant mode of economic development for many American Indian tribes. Casinos generate economic activity in terms of increased population, employment, and housing. Ironically, tribal members may not be the direct recipient of these employment gains. Although employment increases in counties with Native American casinos, most of that growth is due to growth in non-Native American employment. For Native American-owned businesses, the presence of a nearby casino should enhance the opportunities available for the entrepreneurial firm. Most American Indian tribes enforce tribal preferences in hiring and contracting, so the presence of a local casino should increase employment and contracting activity for nearby Native American firms.

Performance and Business Location

In a study of sales revenue and employment within Native American-owned businesses in the US Pacific Northwest, it has been shown that Native American enterprises benefit from their geographic proximity to economic clusters and, in particular, to traded clusters. Specifically, for Native American-owned firms there is a positive relationship between firm revenue and being located proximate to traded economic clusters. This relationship remains strong even when controlling for firm size, firm age, and other environmental factors such as being on a reservation or in an urban area. However, contrary to expectations, no such relationship is found for Native American firms located near local or natural endowment clusters. As traded clusters are made up from traded industries which, by their very nature, generate greater revenues than might be expected with local clusters (defined as local services, such as restaurants and retail), then it should be expected that Native American firms would benefit from being located within traded cluster economies.

Native American entrepreneurs also benefit from geographic proximity to tribally owned gaming venues, in part due to the general preference given to Native American contractors by tribal governments. There is a positive relationship between location near a Tribal gaming venue and the average number of employees within Native American-owned firms, even when controlling for firm revenue and firm age. Proximity to tribal casinos does not lead to more revenue, but it does appear to be beneficial to growth in the number of employees a business is able to sustain. Thus, the data suggest that being close to clusters is good for revenue, while being close to casinos is good for employment.

What Would You Do?

The results of the research create interesting implications for economic development policy within Native American communities. Taken at face value, the results suggests that many Native American firms tend to do better when they are located near economic clusters, in particular to traded economic clusters, which are usually located near urban areas. Firm sales increase when a firm resides in an area with more traded clusters. This presents somewhat of a quandary for many Native American entrepreneurs, who would often prefer to stay on their indigenous grounds, because this can generally only be accomplished by staying on or near the reservation — and most reservations are located in more rural locations. If firms do better when they are located near clusters, how should tribes whose reservation lands are located in rural areas promote entrepreneurial activity?

However, even though overall sales are not statistically different for Native American firms on or off a reservation, firm employment size is. Firms on reservations employ more people than their counterparts off reservations. Moreover, firms located on reservations near tribal casinos grow larger than those that are not. In sum, Native American firms generate better sales revenue near traded cluster economies but experience more employee growth on a reservation and near Native American casinos. Unfortunately, for rural Native American tribes, it may not be possible to be both on the reservation and near economic clusters.

The implications for tribal economic policy are troubling, since there is a trade-off that rural tribes face. Tribes who wish to promote an economic development policy of maximum employment might wish to promote Tribal gaming and keep their businesses on the reservation. On the other hand, Native American entrepreneurs can best increase firm performance by locating their businesses within or near traded cluster economies. However, doing so might require the relocation of the entrepreneur to more urban area, perhaps away from the reservation — a situation that may be culturally abhorrent to many promising Native American entrepreneurs.

It has previously been argued that Native American entrepreneurs face unique challenges associated with their culture and geographic circumstances that might inhibit new business development and performance (Stewart & Schwartz, 2007). Much of the discussion surrounding Tribal gaming has been directed toward the economic impact of casinos on the local economy and public services and, in some cases, upon potential negative unintended consequences that may accompany gaming — for instance, gambling addiction. If Americans Indians are to fully exploit entrepreneurial activity as a means of economic recovery and development, then some thought must be given to the best place to locate new ventures. In addition, the presence and development of tribal entrepreneurship support services (such as tribal banks and training centers) could benefit from having branches serving both rural and urban areas, including on and off the reservation. For those tribes and indigenous entrepreneurs fortunate enough to be located in the vicinity of economic clusters there may be no trade-off. However, for tribes in rural areas, away from traded clusters, the trade-offs may be problematic, since it may be culturally unappealing for those tribes to promote the geographical placement of new tribal ventures and, importantly, their tribal member employees, away from indigenous lands.

Search for Wisdom

— Daniel Stewart & Vincent J. Pascal

Case Questions:

1. Knowing that organizations increase their revenue if they are near economic clusters (which are generally away from American Indian reservations), where would you place your business? What are the trade-offs associated with your choice?

2. Economic clusters are defined as geographic concentrations of firms that offer related or complementary businesses. Given the economic development advantages of clusters, how would you encourage the development of clusters on or near your reservation? What types of activity would facilitate cluster development?

3. Should employment or economic performance be the driving force behind Native American entrepreneurship? Support your position.

Grace Ann's Note

Many thanks to Drs. Stewart and Pascal for this detailed analysis of the kinds of difficult dilemmas facing tribal communities seeking economic development while maintaining tribal integrity! Next, in Part IV, we consider business in relationship to both social and economic sustainability. We begin with a short case about Virginia Maria Romero's public art which brings reminders of wildlife back to the urban landscape which had been their home.

References

Pascal, V. J., & Stewart, D. (2008). The effects of geographic location and economic cluster development on native American entrepreneurship. *International Journal of Entrepreneurship and Innovation, 9*(2), 121−131.

Pascal, V. J., & Stewart, D. (2015). *Native American entrepreneurship: The differential effects of location and tribal gaming.* Working Paper.

Stewart, D., & Schwartz, R. G. (2007). Native American business strategy: A survey of Northwest U.S. firms. *International Journal of Business Performance Management, 9*(3), 259−277.

Part IV
Business Ethics Education in Partnership with the Natural Environment

Remember to Remember: The Alameda Transit Station

Grace Ann Rosile

We recall the words of Greg Cajete, who asks us to "remember to remember" (Cajete, 2015). We have a story to help us remember. This is the story of Virginia Maria Romero, whose art work is on the cover of this book. Her art is also featured in the film series *Tribal Wisdom for Business Ethics*, which is related to this book, and available for free on YouTube or at the New Mexico State University web site: http://business.nmsu.edu/research/programs/daniels-ethics/tribal-ethics/

I (Grace Ann) have known Ginny (Virginia Maria Romero) for many years. She lives here in our town of Las Cruces, NM, and is an internationally recognized artist whose work I have always loved. When I was talking to Ginny about using her art on the cover of this book, she told me this story about her most recent commission.

There was a call for proposals from a group in El Paso (an hour from us) for art to cover the panels of the new Alameda Transit stations (bus stops). The group, the **City of El Paso Museums and Cultural Affairs Department El Paso Public Art Program**, provided background information on the area for the artists making proposals. Of 45 PowerPoint slides with photos of the area, only

2 slides showed only nature, in the form of tree-lined streets and properties. Most photos were of historic architecture. The word "wildlife" did appear once in the call. Despite this seeming emphasis on the man-made aspects of the region, Virginia proposed what she calls her "Urban Wildlife." She told me she always thinks about the wildlife for whom these regions were home before the cities were built. We still see the occasional wild critter in less-concrete-covered places in this part of the country. In our small town, we often hear the beautiful and eerie sound of coyotes yipping and howling at night. Ironically, these real sounds remind us of fake western movie sound effects; but these are real howls from real coyotes, and their sounds remind us to keep our house-cats inside at night.

Ginny sent a sketch of her proposed art work for the El Paso project. She included an explanation that to her, the coyotes and wildlife were also part of the history of the area. She wanted to honor and remember them. They lived on that land before we humans, and some still survive to this day.

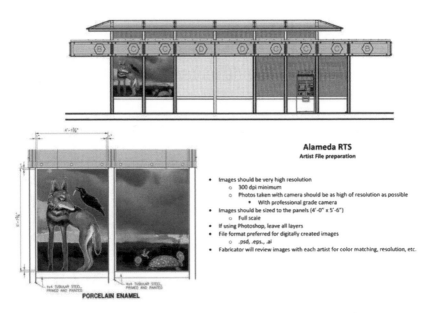

Figure 14.1: Ginny's Submission to City of El Paso Museums and Cultural Affairs Department El Paso Public Art Program.

Virginia was surprised that her proposed art was accepted by the City of El Paso Museums and Cultural Affairs Department El Paso Public Art Program. This organization graciously granted us permission to display the sketches Ginny submitted. You can see them here in Figure 14.1. In addition to being beautiful, these images remind us that we share this planet with other beings, beings whose claim to these lands often predates our own. We have an ethical obligation to respect their rights, and to live in harmony with them, with each other, and with all of nature. These images help us to "remember to remember."

Grace Ann's Note

Many thanks to Virginia Maria Romero for granting permission to tell her story! Her art reminds us to remember the natural world, even in the midst of the demands of modern life.

In the following chapter, Dr. David Boje demonstrates some pitfalls in attempting to measure sustainability using the people-profit-planet scheme of the "Triple Bottom Line." Further, he discusses how a fragmented science of sustainability exists in separate university "silos" of expertise. These silos ignore indigenous and spiritual ecological perspectives, and thus cannot address sustainability adequately. Boje proposes a School of Sustainability to create an effective, holistic approach to sustainability.

Reference

Cajete, G. A. (2015). *Indigenous community: Rekindling the teachings of the seventh fire*. St. Paul, MN: Living Justice Press.

UNIVERSITY OF WINCHESTER
LIBRARY

Critique of the Triple Bottom Line

David M. Boje

The chapter includes a critique of Triple Bottom Line (3BL) sustainability development model (Profit-People-Planet), for reducing everything to a monological measurement of *Profit* as the only measurable, therefore only "real" bottom line. The consequence of the 3BL model is a shallow understanding of the "true" multi-dimensional nature of sustainability from an IWOK (Indigenous Ways-of-Knowing) view. For contribution to theory, I will develop a dialectic approach to how spiritual ecology is being opposed by Western spirituality, which separates People, Planet, and Profit, such as in 3BL. Finally, by way of practical application, I will discuss the formation of a School of Sustainability (SOS) at my university, as a dialectic of thesis (Western spirituality of separation) and antithesis (IWOK of spiritual ecology).

3BL is an example of the monofractal (a recurring self-sameness pattern) carried out to what Alvesson and Spicer (2012, p. 1194) call, functional stupidity: "Functional stupidity refers to an absence of reflexivity, a refusal to use intellectual capacities in other than myopic ways, and avoidance of justifications." 3BL is functional stupidity because it is the traditional sustainability development model dressed up like a fractal, a Sierpinski triangle. The idea is that Economy, Ecology, and Equity, each has bottom lines, and they are in balance.

The 3BL is equity, economy, and ecology, and is sometimes called people, profit, and planet. It is also called cradle-to-cradle organization design (Benkert, 2010; McDonough & Braungart, 2002). Much of the trap of the "Fractal Organization" reasoning is that it only relabels Taylor-Fayol-Weber (TFW) virus, reselling central hierarchic control, and the monologic of profit, to us — essentially old wine in new bottles (Boje, 2015). Norman and MacDonald (2004) are critical of 3BL because of three reasons:

1. 3BL advocates never actually propose how to measure the addition of profit bottom line + People bottom line + Planet bottom line.

2. Without an agreed methodology, the income statement trumps the people and planet measurement.

3. 3BL — does not address how TFW fractal maximizes profit by destroying people and planet.

The functional stupidity written into the game rules of the TFW virus will continue to replicate in modern organizations until we begin to measure the consequences, to measure the dysfunctions of all the functional stupidity.

For Cajete (2015, p. 130) 3BL would be a "surrogate for colonization" and a way to destroy the sustainability crisis by one more progress narrative. The 3BL is missing the "high-context" actuality of the sustainability crisis, and how People and Planet are thoroughly subjugated to Profit, to the monologic that brought on the 2008 foreclosure and banking crisis that is still toppling economies. Some new accounting tools are needed to differentiate the Profit free-for-all, from true "biophysical wealth" (Cajete, 2015, p. 140). Economy, Equity, and Ecology have been out of balance for at least two centuries, and the trend is towards more hegemony, not less. To bring about ecological justice regarding costs, and an Ecology in balance with Equity and Economy is going to take a major paradigm shift.

Next I will give a case example of the dialectic process I am living through at my university, and my attempt at fostering a paradigm shift from Traditional Sustainability Development at the margins, to making the mission of the entire university more sustainable by creating a new SOS. Yes, SOS because the crisis looms, haunts the university and our state.

The SOS Dialectic of Two Spirits

At New Mexico State University (NMSU), I am co-leading the movement to create a SOS. It includes Traditional Environmental Knowledge and IWOK, as a dialectic opposition to unfettered capitalism. The TFW fractal virus of central, top-down, external standards of umpteen agencies and associations is turning the Planet and its Peoples into resources to be used for Profit, while hamstringing the University in its Higher Education and research mission. This TFW virus is turning the University into a Community College, which is already no different from High School and it's No Child Left Behind functional stupidity.

Bringing sustainability consciousness and awareness, let alone action, to NMSU has been a long-term process since 1963, of *interfusing* NMSU *with* those individual moments when the SOS concept has been moving from "abstractions and chimeras" to reality (Hegel, 1807/1977: section #394). Chimera, in Greek mythology, is a monstrous fire-breathing hybrid creature, composed of the parts of more than one animal. Chimera describes sustainability, which means something different to each of the six NMSU colleges, and different to operations, and community. Mostly, until quite recently (with work of Don Pepion in Anthropology and Lisa Greyshield in Education Counseling) it does not mean IWOK, or any sort of spiritual ecology, which some of us are championing. Bringing prominent indigenous scholars Gregory Cajete and Leroy Little Bear to our fourth meeting of the Las Cruces Quantum Storytelling Conference, and featuring them in a university-wide Teaching Academy event, has helped bring awareness.

As yet, however, SOS storytelling has not achieved a harmony, or integrations of all the many disciplines with various perspectives on sustainability, spiritual ecology, Nature, or on the question of how connected are Natural and human domains, and who and what is responsible for climate change, and is climate change real "science" or left wing academic propaganda. Like I said, sustainability is a chimera. As a Hegelian, I am looking for:

> the actualization which is opposed to the initial quiescent being-within-self, an actualization in which "that abstract being-for-self is a being-for-another." Reproduction, however, is the action of this whole introreflected organism, its activity as in itself an End, or as genus, in which the individual repels itself from itself, and in the procreative act reproduces either its organic members or the whole individual. (Hegel, 1807/1977: #266)

But what happens according to Hegelian dialectic is the actualization of spirit beings in non-spirit ways:

> But, as it is, the simple determinateness, qua determinateness of the species, is present in the genus in a non-spiritual manner; actuality starts from the genus, or, what enters into actual existence is not the genus as such, i.e. in general, not the thought of it. (#292)

My own standpoint is to work towards harmony in non-spiritual awareness of the entanglement and integration of all life. And then to include the spiritual, the human domain, and the natural domain, as it comes into actual existence, or spreads from its existence in IWOK. Some of us have a "spiritual purpose" in the SOS project, to harmonize with it (Cajete, 2015, p. 143). SOS, as it comes into some actualization, is a bottom-up initiative. Much of the impetus for signing various sustainability agreements at the top came from pressure of students, bottom-up.

There is dialectic opposition. Traditional university schooling has "targeted Indigenous knowledge for demise" and favored instead a techno-science orientation to sustainability development declaring IWOK as primitive, not consequential, or irrelevant to university science (Cajete, 2015, p. 19). The traditional higher education pedagogy results in:

1. Homogeneity and standardization of the educational experience in reaccreditation outcomes assessment requirements, "making everyone fit into the Western educational mold" (Cajete, 2015, p. 19).

2. A hidden curriculum conditioning faculty and students into the "colonizer view that other ways of knowing are somehow 'less-than', primitive, inconsequential, or mere curiosities in comparison to modern education" (*ibid.*).

3. Higher education continues to be out of balance with the environmental crisis, and yet still perpetuates a very narrow view on "what the earth is," and our role as humans in that world (Cajete, 2015, p. 20).

4. Higher education has become more homogenized, more top-down with its outcome assessment modalities in ways that do not address the "careful adaptation of people to particular places" (Orr & Bowers, cited in p. 20 in Cajete, 2015).

We must address these four aspects of our traditional higher education system before we can create a more collective story of SOS, a way to move beyond the chimera of individual disciplines of what constitutes sustainability. "To live in our distinct lands on Earth" (Cajete, 2015, p. 107): "the stories have helped us understand our place in the world and have formed the foundation of long-term sustainability" (p. 108). For me, this is important because many of the sustainability development efforts to increase recycling, offer micro-loans, etc. are short-term solutions, or band-aids. To create healthy communities in balance with ecology means facing the long-term challenges such as climate change from the population explosion, predominantly meat diet, and the transportation industry.

The emerging guiding story of SOS reflects the university's vision of itself and its future, surviving and sustaining by changing the storyline by "understanding patterns in the world that give meaning to community life and sustain the psychological fabric of a community" (p. 107). The health of the Las Cruces community and New Mexico depends upon how the SOS story functions, and overcomes shallow narratives of sustainability development, rooted in individuality ideologies that are at the expense of a living spiritual ecology.

SOS spiritual ecology answers questions: where we came from, where we can go, what it means to build a sustainable future of higher education, and what it means to be an "Aggie" at our university and to live that story as a living story. It means changing a top-down system of standards applied from accrediting agencies, and silos of separation, so that self-centered teaching and learning are passé. A paradigm shift to interdisciplinary sustainability that has long-term horizons, across multiple generations, is called for. This is contrary to the "rugged individuality" of what it means to be an American on their individualized Hero's Journey to fame and riches. The American rags-to-riches Hero's Journey has many high costs built into it, but no boon returned to the community.

Rather than McMansions and over-consumption, SOS spiritual ecology means simplicity in ways of housing, food, and transportation. The alternative is collapsing ecology, species extinction, increases in diabetes from processed food diets, the concentration of wealth in the .001 percent, while 50 percent of the world's population lives on less than $2 a day. In the United States, almost a third of the work force is contingent, not contract labor. Most Americans are two missed paychecks away from homelessness, and estimates are there are as many as 3.5 million Americans homeless. Already there are worldwide refuges from broken economies and a succession of wars to the point some nations are always at war somewhere.

The SOS could therefore integrate IWOK and develop ecological literacy across the country, bring social as well as environmental justice to our communities, change the storyline of the state of New Mexico and of the nation. This would have the advantage of students obtaining deeper understanding of the relationship and interdependence between their sustainability knowledge and their choice of livelihood, and how the two are related. Faculty and students would learn to live a story of interdependent life with the Natural world, rather than living a story of individuality, typical of the rags-to-riches entrepreneurial Horatio Alger myth. The individuality story is unfolding more readily at NMSU and most universities in the United States, given the silos colleges form, making interdisciplinary approaches to sustainability a challenge.

Leadership is needed, way to help the university go through the paradigm shift. "A leadership program must help leaders learn to sustain and perpetuate our communities through time and the ebb and flow of available resources" (Cajete, 2015, p. 181). It involves a shift from TFW fractal virus, call it bureaucracy mixed with standardizing every university process everywhere, but to what? Can a state university unlearn bureaucracy, exit from the mechanistic time and motion study of faculty and student performance, and change the administrative order it is so used to performing? We are talking about not only a shift from TFW mindset, but a shift in habits of action.

Faculty hunger, I think, for such a paradigm shift. Students, I believe, are hungering to live stories in their place on the earth, in their life grounded in sense of place, a sense of community involvement, and ecological answerability and even spiritual ecology. Spiritual ecology is opposed by Western forms of spirituality that separate this world from the world of the afterlife, and separate human from Nature, which leads to treating Nature as a resource for exploitation.

I will say it: we need "spiritual leaders of the environmental movement" who can incorporate traditional Indigenous practices (Cajete, 1999, p. 19) with current sustainability science. This spiritual ecology type of leadership builds relationships within a community, fostering a balance with ecological capacity, and a sense of living within the cycles of Nature (Cajete, 2000).

Traditional science practices often deny "animal rights" calling it form of "animism" but there is much we can learn from animals.

Humans recognizing animal rights is step towards posthumanism (Barad, 2007), decentering the human standpoint, and developing ecological awareness that we are one of many animal species, living interdependently with plants, and all kinds of microbiological life. Sometimes one needs a high-powered microscope to see all these life forms. Cajete (2000, p. 261) reminds us that spiritual ecology is the basis of Native Science.

A Shift in Critical Pedagogy to a Critical Ecological Pedagogy

There are pockets of Friere's (1970) *Pedagogy of the Oppressed*, such as in the Curriculum and Instruction department in NMSU's College of Education. There one finds a community-based focus on working with communities to deal with social, economic, and political oppression, using talking circles to aid the community to express their concerns to power. However, I would agree with Cajete (2015, p. 71) that Friere's model does not include ecology. It needs to go deeper to include the Natural world to arrive at a "sustainable process of education." This is precisely what we hope to achieve with SOS, to bring to the fore, how "divorcing human peoples from the natural world has proven disastrous" (Cajete, 2015, p. 77).

Paradigm Shift to Dialectic Model of Sustainability

Sustainability is a chimera. "These have vanished, being abstractions and chimeras belonging to those first shallow shapes of spiritual self-consciousness, and having their truth only in the imaginary being of the heart, in imagination and rhetoric, not in Reason" (Hegel, 1807/1977, #394). Nevertheless the Hegelian chimera-SOS is moving from the shallow shapes of its "spiritual self-consciousness." SOS and spiritual ecology existed initially only in the imaginary being of the heart-of-care, in our storytelling rhetoric and imagination, but not yet in the science "Reason" of NMSU.

Spiritual, here, refers to "school spirit" of an institution. Reason, here, refers to the various rationalities of NMSU, its sciences, operations, administrative order, its students, faculty, and staff. All these different Rationalities constellate NMSU-Reason. Appendix A gives a brief history of milestones in the formation of the chimera-SOS moving from shallow shapes of its "spiritual consciousness" into the storytelling and the "Reason"-rationalities of NMSU.

How is the spiritual coming into being at NMSU? For Hegel, spirituality takes on truly real substance, after coming into self-conscious awareness, then the substance of action can emerge:

> In the "matter in hand", then, in which the interfusion of individuality and objectivity has itself become objective, self-consciousness has come into possession of its true Notion, or has attained to a consciousness of its substance. At the same time, this consciousness as it exists here is one that has just now come into being, and hence is an immediate consciousness of its substance; and this is the specific way in which spiritual being is present here; it has not yet developed into a truly real substance. (Hegel, 1807/1977, #411)

The substantive changes come slowly. A paradigm shift towards sustainability began in 1963 faculty research. Then in 2004, at the insistence of students, NMSU established a Climate Change Task Force. In 2007 NMSU signed the American College of University Presidents Climate Commitment, and declared 2009 the "Year of Sustainability" at NMSU, and signed the Talloires agreement. In 2011 Faculty Senate created a memorial to establish the Office of Sustainability and support a Sustainability Council. This led to gathering the 250 pages of metrics to claim a Bronze (2011) then a Gold Star (2012) in Sustainability. This has given momentum to the Greening the Curriculum initiative, and now to SOS.

When the President's Performance Fund provided support for the Greening the Curriculum (December 17, 2013), we finally had a budget and legitimacy to initiate sustainability minors across the six colleges of main campus. This Spiral Development plan was part of the proposal, and served as an implementation strategy (Figure 15.1).

The Spiral of Development begins with the NMSU Gold Star rating from AASHE (November 30, 2012) and ends with SOS formation (still in process).

- **1st Teaching Academy: September 16 2013** — Rani Alexander convened a Teaching Academy session on Sustainability Across the Curriculum of NMSU, I got nominated at that meeting to put together a funding application to the President's Performance Fund from the Sustainability Council. This "Greening the Curriculum" proposal was due in two weeks. At the Teaching Academy meeting: Mark Andersen; Rani Alexander; Candace Gilfillan; M. Stanford; Christopher Brown; Steven Loring; Abbas Ghassemi; William Lindemann; Constance Falk; Mark Uchanski; Jean Conway; joni newcomer. David Boje obtained valuable support and assistance into developing the funding proposal from this group that would get the "Green Leaf" into the catalogue and course schedule. The Greening the Curriculum proposal did get funded on December 17, 2013. On January 8, 2014, several motions were passed at Sustainability Council, and David Boje was made *Coordinator* to *Greening the Curriculum* initiative.

- **2nd Teaching Academy: December 2015** — David Boje, Coordinator for Greening the Curriculum, and incoming Chair of Sustainability Council, convened a Teaching Academy session to create a "SOS" at NMSU. David Boje, Lois Stanford, and Mark Uchanski presented the vision of SOS and the participants came up with ideas of action, and agreed to move forward with SOS, by developing a retreat at NMSU sometime in May 2016 where Foundation people, Provost, Dean of Graduate School, potential donors, and Sustainability Council would go in this retreat in May 2016. One of the key ideas was to include a strong focus on Native

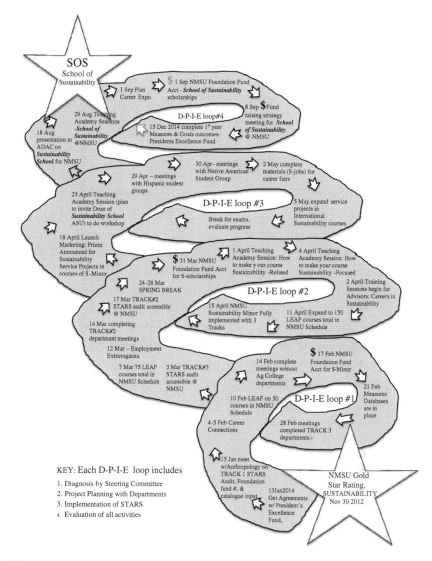

Figure 15.1: Spiral of Development of SOS, from the January 13, 2014 Agreement on President's Excellence Fund, Academic Associate Deans Council (ADAC), and Office of Institutional Analysis (OIA).

Ways of Knowing, which is the topic of a conference held at NMSU in May (Lisa Greyshield).

- **3rd Teaching Academy: February 18 2016** — 2:35–3:50 pm in Milton room 50 for purpose of planning the SOS retreat, briefing Provost, Dean of Graduate School, Deans of colleges and their development officers, and Foundation people, and potential donors participate in May 2016, on the main campus (Lisa Greyshield's conference on Native Ways of Knowing).

The "Heart of Care" for sustainability, despite its chimeras, was presented to President and Provost in 2011, but without IWOK (Figure 15.2).

This figure was the focus of a May 2011 presentation to the former President Couture and Provost Wilkins of NMSU by David Boje of Sustainability Council, his doctoral students, and joni newcomer of Office of Sustainability.

NMSU mainstream higher education has promoted a separation of humans from the natural world, and especially separation of spirit and nature. I know in my own department of management, humans are treated as "resources" to organizations. When I started teaching, way back in the mid-1970s, the field was called,

Figure 15.2: "Heart-of-Care" and Various Shades of Green Sustainability "School Spirit" in the Operations, Research, Education, and Community of NMSU.

"personnel." Once personnel became "human resource management," it was game over.

One aim of the SOS project is to foster "sustainability, survival, and life-supporting respect for all that is" (Cajete, 2015, p. 77). Including IWOK is a way to bring an inclusive, holistic, community-oriented alternative to the narratives of globalization and Western sustainability development models. Rebuilding and revitalizing community sustainability means we "live by healthy core values that will sustain life" (*ibid.*). It is the kind of way of living one's living story that SOS *with* IWOK can bring about.

Conclusions

A dialectic analysis of SOS implementation reveals a struggle of opposition between many kinds of spirtualties: the Ascendant spirituality where this world we live in is separated from the after world, the Pope's call for Catholics to be stewards of the natural world and do something to curb climate change, a survival of the fittest spirituality (Spencerism) in which the rich are meant to be rich and the poor to be poor, a spiritual ecology where everything has an animated spiritual energy, and so on.

From 1963 to present, with the series of moments of sustainability initiatives (Appendix A) as storyline, a community story of a SOS is emerging. It is not widely shared; in fact, at this writing, it is mostly unknown. But 33 radio ads, and a Ted-Talk-styled gathering in February, and another Teaching Academy event to plan the SOS retreat, will bring greater awareness across the campus. If a deep-pockets donor can be found, who knows, the SOS can actualize more quickly, and the paradigm shift will gain administrative momentum.

The world faces one crisis of sustainability after another, so the rhetoric of denial and *laissez faire* unfettered capitalism is harder for the public to swallow. The sustainability narrative of progress is harder to defend; even the apologists are not that passionate about it. On Talk Radio the climate change is propaganda, naysayers are still persuading most Americans to deny the data, and instead accept a distorted storyline of what is happening to Mother Earth.

SOS needs to hold a space/place, and a time for story-making where separation is questioned, and the nested nature of individual, community, and ecology are seen as interdependent with entanglements that are explored. The function of SOS storying and story-making is to make sustainable communities that survive and sustain in a place through time (Cajete, 2015, p. 107).

> Western society must once again become nature-centered. (Cajete, 2000, p. 266)

References

Aguirre, G., Boje, D. M., Cast, M. L., Conner, S. L., Helmuth, C., Mittal, R., & Yan, T. Q. (2012). University sustainability and system ontology. *International Journal of Organization Theory and Behavior*, *15*(4), 577–618.

Alvesson, M., & Spicer, A. (2012). A stupidity-based theory of organizations. *Journal of Management Studies*, *49*(7), 1194–1220.

Barad, K. (2007). *Meeting the universe halfway: Quantum physics and the entanglement of matter and meaning*. Durham, NC: Duke University Press.

Benkert, M. (2010). *Architect as developer: A model for triple top line development*. Doctoral dissertation, University of Cincinnati, Cincinnati, OH.

Boje, D. M. (2015). Mapping quantum storytelling fractal patterns before and beneath triple bottom line's and veterans administration's stupid narratives. *Proceedings of big story conference*, December 17–19, 2015, Los Angeles.

Cajete, G. (1999). *A people's ecology: Explorations in sustainable living*. Book Marketing Group.

Cajete, G. (2000). *Native science: Natural laws of interdependence*. Santa Fe, NM: Clear Light Publishers.

Cajete, G. A. (2015). *Indigenous community: Rekindling the teachings of the seventh fire*. St. Paul, MN: Living Justice Press.

Friere, P. (1970). *Pedagogy of the oppressed*. New York, NY: Continuum.

Hegel, G. W. F. (1807/1977). *Phenomenology of spirit*. (A. V. Miller, Trans., Foreword by J.N. Findlay; First published in German, 1806; English 1977. Oxford, NY: Oxford University Press.

McDonough, W., & Braungart, M. (2002). Design for the triple top line: New tools for sustainable commerce. *Corporate Environmental Strategy, 9*(3), 251–258.

Norman, W., & MacDonald, C. (2004). Getting to the bottom of "triple bottom line". *Business Ethics Quarterly, 14*(2), 243–262.

APPENDIX A:
A BRIEF HISTORY OF NMSU SUSTAINABILITY —
see more complete history at http://davidboje. com/sustainability/history.htm

- 1963–2003 — various sustainability-related institutes, grants, initiatives, and faculty research publications.

- 2004 — NMSU President Michael V. Martin establishes "The Sustainability and Climate Change Task Force" headed by Robert Moulton to deal with rising energy prices and climate commitment.

- 2007 — NMSU President Michael V. Martin signs the American College of University Presidents Climate Commitment (ACUPCC), making NMSU a charter signatory.

  - College of Engineering beings offering a renewable energy technologies minor.

  - NMSU moves to utilizing greener transportation.

  - An alliance to develop wind research facility is established.

- 2009 — Interim President Waded Cruzado-Salas declares 2009 the "Year of Sustainability" and signed Talloires Declaration of the Association of University Leaders for a Sustainable Future.

- February 2011 — Faculty Senate Bill, which passed unanimously on February 19, 2011, and recognized the new Office of Sustainability at NMSU and supported the plans and goals of the Sustainability Council.

- May 2011 — joni newcomer, professor Connie Falk, David Boje's entire systems theory doctoral seminar (Mgt 655), made a presentation to President Couture, Provost Wilkins, and VP of Research, Vimal Chaitanya, about the history interviews we had conducted with sustainability leaders (the little people) at NMSU, and the ways that sustainability fits into all seven goals of the university (see published article on study of sustainability and this meeting by Aguirre, Grant; Boje, David M.; Cast, Melissa L.; Conner, Suzanne L.; Helmuth, Catherine; Mittal, Rakesh; Saylors, Rohny; Tourani, Nazanin; Vendette, Sebastien; Aguirre et al., 2012).

- 2011 — NMSU earned a prestigious Bronze Star rating for its sustainability from AASHE.

- November 30, 2012 — NMSU earned a Gold Star rating from AASHE for its sustainability.

- April 16, 2013 — NMSU receives Bicycle Friendly University designation.

- **1st Teaching Academy: September 16 2013** — Rani Alexander convened a Teaching Academy session on Sustainability Across the Curriculum of NMSU, I got nominated at that meeting to put together a funding application to the President's Performance Fund from the Sustainability Council. This "Greening the Curriculum" proposal was due in two weeks. At the Teaching Academy meeting: Mark Andersen; Rani Alexander; Candace Gilfillan; M. Stanford; Christopher Brown; Steven Loring; Abbas Ghassemi; William Lindemann; Constance Falk; Mark Uchanski; Jean Conway; joni newcomer. David Boje obtained valuable support and assistance into developing the funding proposal from this group that would get the "Green Leaf" into the catalogue and course schedule. The Greening the Curriculum proposal did get funded on December 17, 2013. On January 8, 2014, several motions were passed at Sustainability Council, and David Boje was made *Coordinator* to *Greening the Curriculum* initiative.

- **2nd Teaching Academy: December 2015** — David Boje, Coordinator for Greening the Curriculum, and incoming Chair of Sustainability Council, convened a Teaching Academy session to create a "SOS" at NMSU.

Search for Wisdom

— Dr. Grace Ann Rosile

Universities experience controversy over how to make sustainability an integral part of the curriculum. Arguments are made for social or environmental sustainability to be a component of many classes across campus, as a key feature of every existing discipline. Others favor whole courses dedicated specifically to social or environmental sustainability, whole majors or minors, or an entire "SOS."

1. What are the pros and cons of each alternative: a topic within many courses, or else dedicated courses in distinct majors and programs?

2. Can you think of other alternatives besides these two approaches? Explain.

3. What do you see as the best way to embed sustainability into university curriculums?

4. Most elementary schools already teach children about recycling. What role, if any, should the University have in these efforts to reach children at such young ages?

5. What role should businesses have in changing people's views of sustainability?

Grace Ann's Note

Many thanks to David Boje for contributing this important critique of 3BL! He has demonstrated that worthwhile goals and good intentions are not enough. We also need realistic critiques of how we measure our steps towards those goals. Then we need integrated university structures to create integrated holistic approaches to sustainability.

Next, we translate Boje's systemic concerns into personal impacts. Dr. Gerri Elise McCulloh offers a personal account of social and environmental effects of tourism, and the impact of national protection policies, on historic American Indian sacred sites.

16

Songs of the Pika and Others at the Bighorn Medicine Wheel

Gerri Elise McCulloh

Mountain Pika, small mountain rodents thought to be close genetic relatives of the rabbit, live in rock outcroppings in the Bighorn Mountains. Extremely susceptible to climate change, dust, development, and other pressures, the mountain Pika are fast overtaking the polar bear as the symbol for species extinction from runaway pressures in the Anthropocene. Often bearing only one or two offspring, their numbers are hard to replenish once logging roads or mountain towns have destroyed their habitat. Additionally, some species only travel one-half mile in their lifetimes, making recovery slow when their populations are stressed. Most live above tree lines and prefer cold quiet areas. They are gatherers of wildflowers and grasses, and build haystacks within their rocky burrows. Often, the outside of their burrows look decorated, as they carefully dry wildflowers and grasses in preparation to stack so mold does not harm their winter food supply.

Mountain Pika once flourished at the Bighorn Medicine Wheel. About 50 years ago their songs and whistles sang people to the top of Medicine Mountain on a series of trails that crisscrossed the mountain. This was before the road was built in the 1970s to carry tourists to the top. Few remember their songs, but the Pika were my playmates on the side of Medicine Mountain and their songs and whistles are embedded deep within my bones and cells as memories carrying a way of knowing few remember and even fewer share.

Medicine Mountain and the surrounding areas, including Porcupine Falls, Bear Mountain, the Agate Cliffs, and of course the Bighorn Medicine Wheel, are all sacred places from my childhood. My grandfather, an Osage-Chickasaw-Scottish sheepherder grazed our sheep every spring in the Bighorn Mountains. Our sheep camp was a little more than a mile northeast of Medicine Mountain. In those days there was a back road, a commonly washed out jeep trial, that came along the backside and wound like a snake up Medicine Mountain to the top, where the Medicine Wheel and the upper cliffs could be seen. Sometime in the 1930s President Roosevelt had the Civil Conservation Corps (CCC) build a small rock wall along the cliffs. I remember as a young woman I would sit on the wall to watch the golden eagles fly below me. Their nests were on the cliffs below, where they raised their chicks. This rock wall is now gone.

When I think about the sacred places of my childhood, the words of Belden C. Lane echo meaningfully. He said there are four axioms western thinkers must understand about sacred places, "The first such axiom is that the *sacred place is not chosen, it chooses.*" (Lane, 2002, p. 19, emphasis in original). This means the sacred place is so alive it communicates something necessary, indeed healing, to those who encounter the place ready to hear. Often this sacredness is a chorus, joined and performed by non-human inhabitants of the living landscape. Animals living at sacred sites are so important, Vine Deloria Jr. states:

> We might even say that the sacredness of the lands extends to and is apprehended by other forms of life. Without their presence the land would lack an important dimension. Not only is the presence of other forms of life necessary for the land, it is sometimes the determining factor in identifying sacred locations. (Deloria, 1999, p. 258)

In days before the roads, many participants of the living environment, including the rocks, wind, wildflowers, bear, pika, and golden eagles, joined in a chorus to announce the sacred lessons that could be learned at Medicine Mountain. While those lessons are not mine to teach, I think sharing my memories of the songs of Medicine Mountain might give visitors a deeper, richer experience should they visit.

In the next section I want to describe the physical place or the material space that constitutes the Bighorn Medicine Wheel so an image of how the terrain is now navigated by visitors may be visualized. I do this acutely aware of deficiencies produced by textual description. Nevertheless, having an image of the various physical compositions will lay a foundation for talking about how the identities (plural) of the Bighorn Medicine Wheel are now offered to the public. I will later address some of the compositions at the site that perform a chorus for profound learning. Some of this essay has been adapted from my dissertation research (McCulloh, 2015).

Recent Background Tones Contributing to the Songs Now Expressed

In 1988 the US Forest Service planned to develop the Bighorn Medicine Wheel for tourism, proposing a parking lot and large visitor's center at the summit, including a viewing platform jutting over the wheel so visitors could ponder the wheel from above. This plan was widely contested by Native Americans and others. In 1989 the Medicine Wheel Coalition for Sacred Sites of North America was formed along with the Medicine Wheel Alliance to fight the US Forest Service plan. In October 1996 the parties adopted a long-term plan to manage the site called the Historic Preservation Plan for the Medicine Wheel National Historic Landmark and Medicine Mountain (HPP), effectively setting aside between 18,000 and 20,000 acres as an area for consultation with the five tribes that constituted the Medicine Wheel Coalition: Arapaho, Shoshone, Blackfoot, Northern Cheyenne, and Crow.

Justice Holloway, writing in the United States Court of Appeals, Tenth Circuit decision (D.C. No.99-CV-0031-J), rendered September 2004, regarding the management of the Medicine Wheel gives a good description of the ancient stone structure:

> The Medicine Wheel National Historic Landmark was created in 1969 to preserve the Medicine Wheel, a prehistoric stone circle about 80 feet in diameter that was constructed by the aboriginal peoples of North America. The wheel includes a large cairn in the center and 28 radiating spokes of rocks. Although the age of the structure is unknown, archeological evidence indicates that human presence in the area goes back for 7,500 years or more. Many tepee rings, trails, and other artifacts and traces of human habitation are found in the vicinity. A number of Native American tribes consider the Wheel to be sacred. (US Court of Appeals, Tenth Circuit, D.C. No.99-CV-0031-J, p. 2)

Both the court decision and the HPP specifically state that US Forest Service management "ensures that the Medicine Wheel and Medicine Mountain are managed in a manner that protects the integrity of the site as *a sacred site* and a *nationally important traditional cultural property*" (US Court of Appeals, Tenth Circuit, D.C. No.99-CV-0031-J, p. 4, emphasis added). The court ensured that any changes at the Bighorn Medicine Wheel were to be reviewed by the Medicine Wheel Coalition, the US Forest Service, and the Federal Aviation Administration before implementation.

Entangled Melodies

The geology at the summit of Medicine Mountain is an unusual protrusion of Archaean Eon rock that is part of continental core rock or continental nuclei. This continental nuclei rock formed just after the collision that formed earth's moon, some 4.5 billion years ago. It is the first rock of a living planet. The Bighorn Medicine Wheel is situated on top of the most ancient of Earth's geological formations.

Ancient people built a stone circle approximately 80 feet in diameter on top of the birth-rock of the planet. Within the stone circle is a central cairn with 28 radiating stone spokes. Located along the circle's perimeter are six stone Cairns, or dugouts with rock linings, bringing the total number of Cairns at this site to seven.

Significantly, the Archaean Eon rock outcroppings, the continental nuclei, occur along the Rockies up into the Canadian Saskatchewan Mountains. There are upwards of 162 known ancient rock medicine wheels and the Bighorn Medicine Wheel is arguably the best known of these ancient structures in the United States.

Courtney Milne (1999) has photographed the Bighorn Medicine Wheel and used it as a central map, extending each of its 28 spokes outward and mapping at least two sacred sites lining up with each spoke. His investigation of the corresponding 52 sacred indigenous sites are interesting, but for my purposes, I want to start with visitor's first encounters, to tease out the narratives and stories being performed there.

Only a few elders and disabled are allowed to drive to the summit, so most visitors arrive and park about a mile and a half away and walk to the top. A tiny visitor's center with maps and restrooms are below, now often staffed by volunteers from the indigenous tribes in the area. These volunteers sometimes act as interpretive guides and can give great insights into the surrounding tipi rings and other artifacts in the area so visitors know what to look for as they walk up the road to the summit.

Although indigenous sacred traditions are not homogenous and engage a wide diversity of practices, medicine wheels in general represent the regenerative cycles of life emanating from Mother Earth joining with Father Sky. Barbara Alice Mann, a noted Seneca scholar states, "Mother Earth is clearly among the *most ancient* of Native ideas" (Mann, 2006, p. 127, emphasis in original). It is important to understand some of the basic meanings of medicine wheels, including their signifying structures from this matriarchal vantage point.

Medicine wheels are circles that do not have beginnings or ends; they represent infinity, cycles, and the entanglements of all life. Medicine wheels are usually separated into even quadrants representing the cardinal directions. At the Bighorn Medicine

Wheel, stone lines mark East and West, North, and South. The six directions of East, South, West, North, Above, and Below, locate participants in relation to the center within, which is the seventh point, the axis, where all other points meet. Together these signify the creation and creator/creatrix in relation and interrelatedness. Importantly, as Trudy Sable notes, "You cannot speak of Creator as something that has already happened, such as 'When God created the world'. God is a process, a continuously manifesting creative force" (Sable, 2006, p. 169). The process and cycles of life are preeminent in medicine wheel structures.

Sacred Numbers of the Bighorn Medicine Wheel

The Bighorn Medicine Wheel, with 28 radiating spokes, large central Cairn and 6 peripheral Cairns may also represent astronomical events visible during the summer months. The 28 spokes are thought to relate to the lunar cycle and other astronomical cycles. One of the outer Cairns aligns with sunrise at the summer solstice. Additionally, two major stars, one rising 28 days before summer solstice and the other rising 28 days after summer solstice are located by two peripheral Cairns (Eddy, 1974/2007; Robinson, 2007). The number 28 is also significantly feminine, representing a woman's menstrual cycle and the lunar cycles.

Furthermore, there are 28 spokes that, when divided by the four cardinal directions, leaves seven spokes per quadrant. With 28 radiating spokes, seven in each quadrant, seven is signified in all aspects of the Bighorn Medicine Wheel. Seven is the number of the ancient virgin, not because of abstinence from sexual relations, but because of the quality of non-repeatability. Seven-sided geometrical figures require unequal angles to close the figure. If one were to use perfectly equal angles to draw a heptagon, the result would be an open spiral. Heptagons must have at least one approximated angle to materialize.

The musical reflection of seven is the scale, repeated only at higher octaves, and therefore not comprised of seven identical repeating tones. This non-repeatability may also be understood as mimetic moments in hermeneutics. The virgin or goddess in Paleolithic and Neolithic Europe was often represented as a spiral symbolizing generative matter but not perfectly repeatable time. In Greece the number seven represented an aspect of a Creatrix and the energy or creative harmony of creation time, understood by the ancient Greeks as rebalancing *kairos* time (McCulloh, 2015).

The central cairn of the Bighorn Medicine Wheel may be seen as a focal point for practice, prayer, and ceremony and may be looked upon during ceremony as the dynamic relations from which all else emanates, spirals and whorls; the living place with power to rebalance all else. The definition of the *center* in physics is the point at or through which a force is considered to act. When we speak of center as the *center* of gravity we mean the spot of equilibrium. The central Cairn at the Big Horn Medicine Wheel is a reminder of both emanating life force and equilibrium or balance necessary for regenerative relations.

Finally, Medicine Wheels are sacred spaces for ceremony. Most indigenous people enter medicine wheels at the east and immediately travel south along the perimeter. A few warrior and Sundance societies enter medicine wheels at the west and travel clockwise along the perimeter. Otherwise, East is the traditional direction for ceremonial entry into a lodge or medicine wheel.

When practicing within a Sundance society at the *Pe' Sla* in South Dakota, I learned about a constellation that is also a medicine wheel. This constellation is almost directly overhead in the northern hemisphere in the summer and is translated loosely as the lodge of the creator. The door of the constellation rotates until, at the summer solstice, the door to the lodge is facing east and is said to be open. Again, each tribe has constellations and practices that differ from one another, but medicine wheels signify cyclical, nonlinear creation time that may be engaged and activated in practice and ceremony.

Deloria suggests that institutionalization often leaves the state in charge, and at sacred sites that also double as sites for cultural tourism this may mark a dangerous juncture since, "when the sacred hoops of life were broken, thousands of years ago for non-Indians and a century ago for most Indians, the possibility of recapturing that original sense of awe and respect was lost and could not be recovered" (Deloria, 1999, p. 267). Thus, unless we can somehow re-member transformations from cellular memories holding multiple and fluid pasts and futures, we limit the songs we can learn to harmonize with.

UNIVERSITY OF WINCHESTER LIBRARY

> ## Other Medicine Wheels
>
> Medicine wheels are not confined to the Americas. Gimbutas (1982, 1989, 1991) in her research shows the designs of circles with directional spokes were motifs in thousands of artifacts including Paleolithic and Neolithic pottery in ancient Europe; settlements were also often shaped in circles with the cardinal directions marked. Gimbutas asserts ancient medicine wheel symbols always signified beginnings and becoming in generative cycles.

Songs of Roads, Fences, and Guards

When visitors walk to the summit of Medicine Mountain to view the Bighorn Medicine Wheel, they journey along a wide road traversing the saddleback of the mountain. Signage guides them, sometimes giving information about the geography and geology. Upon reaching the road to the summit, along the west, the hundreds of trails, crisscrossing up the slope of the mountain are gone, as are the mountain Pika that made them. Now the road allows for one way of looking and one way of understanding the journey. This single perspective narrative reduces and limits the experience and echoes with a linear progress disconnected from generative non-linear creation.

Upon reaching the summit, a groomed trail and a fence surround the medicine wheel. Conceptually, what is a fence, but a way of keeping in or out that which the narrative says should not mix? The fence simultaneously includes and excludes as a boundary. Additionally, the material fence around the medicine wheel is constructed with an entrance at the Northwest. Native American practitioners who use the medicine wheel in ceremonies usually crawl through the fence at the east to enter according to ceremonial custom. Thankfully the HPP was specified in writing as a living document, so future changes may be made eventually. This fence made of wood and rope, as troubling as it is, is far better than the first fence, built of metal, that effectively kept out most Native Americans, since metal at or in ceremonial lodges or spaces is prohibited in many tribes. The fence echoes a history of government, social, and cultural oppression and marginalization of indigenous people and their perspectives. These echoes add to the tones of the chorus now heard on Medicine Mountain, but if you listen closely, the echoes of challenges to the doctrines of discovery may also be heard. Since the Bighorn Medicine Wheel is built upon the oldest continental core rock, a song of birth and rebirth in generative cycles is amplified. Remember, medicine wheels are symbols of becoming and creation or generative time. The resonating symbols move listeners into contemplation of the most ancient birth rock of the planet toward a profound melody of renewing cycles and lively hope.

Nevertheless, the fence in consumerist narratives acts to empty out the subject of harmonious creation in what is tantamount to a chastity belt disallowing fructification and birth. Within the song of eco- and cultural tourism, an imposed abjection is produced. Abject space is that space that is between object and subject and constitutes a condition that is not quite alive. First noted by William Apess in the 1820s in *An Indian's Looking-Glass For the White Man* (1992), abject space represents the space where those who are forced to the periphery dwell without voice or hope of coherence in the dominant social space, spatial economy or within the dominant narrative (see also Boje, 2008). The fence in this consuming cultural tourism signifies a border and a boundary, man-made, limiting, and linear, to keep the significance of the Bighorn Medicine Wheel, and her song of continual regeneration, muted for those who have not known creation's songs.

Outside the fence, a uniformed US Forest Service guide or guard stands at north. The echoes of military action are signified in the uniform itself; authority to guard creation echoes patriarchal linear history, erasing details of renewing and renewable stories. The guard now acts to enforce who may or may not enter the fenced area. Those who are admitted must show proper proof they are Native American or be part of a Native American group scheduled for ceremony. Many indigenous people are not allowed to enter the Bighorn Medicine Wheel to pray, so they leave prayer offerings on the fence or toss their offerings inside.

In the cultural tourism narrative, the prayers tied to the fence around the wheel become a consumed spectacle in an institutionalized practice the US Forest Service controls. One cannot help but notice that given the oppression of indigenous people the world over, an exotically adorned fence echoes into narratives of oppression because histories and the sacred hoops that bind them are not understood as living testaments of hope, but rather are relegated to the outside of living generative creation. Nevertheless, strains of another song are also apparent. Material offerings of celebration, reverence, and awe cover the boundary that simultaneously includes and excludes, revealing a generative creation song at the Bighorn Medicine Wheel that cannot be muted by a fence or a guard.

The great Laguna poet, Paula Gunn Allen (1999) said, "the root of oppression is the loss of memory". While the mountain Pika no longer whistle and sing on Medicine Mountain to guide people up to the summit, perhaps my offering of honor and reverence and awe in this book on Tribal Wisdom is the memory of their guiding songs. When the mountain Pika acted as the guides to the Bighorn Medicine Wheel, there were also hundreds of trails on the side of the mountain. No journey to the summit was ever the same. As a child, I followed the songs and whistles, traversing from clan to clan as I made my way up Medicine Mountain. Sometimes I even crossed my own trail to head toward the base again, then back up, always following the songs that eventually called me to the summit to enter the Bighorn Medicine Wheel and join the chorus of generative creation time.

Search for Wisdom

1. Tribal peoples had to climb through a fence at Bighorn Medicine Wheel, in order to enter in proper ceremonial fashion from the east. Is this situation OK? What makes a fence good or bad?

2. How can we balance the need for protection (of land, resources, sacred sites) with the need and desire of people to visit these places? (*Note*: this same dilemma affects all National Parks and National Monuments.)

3. Do we care enough, or too much, about disappearing species? Do we care enough, or too much, about disappearing human cultures? Are these two issues related? Explain.

4. What, if any, are the similarities and differences between American Indian sacred sites in nature, and Euro-Western holy shrines and churches?

Grace Ann's Note

Many thanks to Dr. Gerri McCulloh for this first-hand account of changes witnessed within her lifetime, along with historical details of this important sacred site! This chapter has taken us from Boje's focus on systemic levels of change, to McCulloh's focus on person and place. Next we move to Kaylynn Sullivan TwoTrees and Matthew Kolan's experiences at the interpersonal level, as a model for creating a sustainable interpersonal and business relationships.

References

Allen, P. G. (1999). Who is your mother?: Red roots of white feminism. In C. Lemert (Ed.), *Social theory: The multicultural and classic readings* (pp. 585–593). Boulder, CO: Westview Press, The Perseus Books Group.

Apess, W. (1992). *On our own ground: The complete writings of William Apess*. Amherst, MA: University of Massachusetts Press.

Boje, D. M. (2008). *Storytelling organizations*. London: Sage.

Deloria, V. (1999). *For this land: Writings on religion in America*. New York, NY: Routledge.

Eddy, J. D. (1974/2007). *Solar-Center*. Stanford University Website. Retrieved from http://solar-center.stanford.edu/AO/bighorn.html. Accessed on October 10, 2007.

Gimbutas, M. (1982). *The goddesses and gods of old Europe: 6500-3500BC: Myths and cult images: New and updated edition*. Berkeley, CA: University of California Press.

Gimbutas, M. (1989). *The language of the goddess*. New York, NY: Harper and Row Publishers.

Gimbutas, M. (1991). *The civilization of the goddess*. San Francisco, CA: HarperCollins.

Lane, B. C. (2002). *Landscapes of the sacred: Geography and narrative in American spirituality*. Baltimore, MD: Johns Hopkins University Press.

Mann, B. A. (2006). Where are your women? Missing in action. In D. T. Jacobs (Ed.), *Unlearning the language of conquest: Scholars expose anti-Indianism in America*. Austin, TX: University of Texas Press.

McCulloh, G. E. (2015). *Toward an acoustic rhetoric: Vital materialism's diffractions*. Doctoral dissertation, New Mexico State University, ProQuest.

Milne, C. (1999). *Sacred places in North America: A journey into the medicine wheel*. New York, NY: Stewart, Tabori & Chang Publishing.

Robinson. (2007). *Solar-Center*. Stanford University Website. Retrieved from http://solar-center.stanford.edu/AO/bighorn.html. Accessed on October 10, 2007.

Sable, T. (2006). Preserving the whole: Principles of sustainability in Mi'kmaw forms of communication. In D. T. Jacobs (Ed.), *Unlearning the language of conquest: Scholars expose anti-Indianism in America*. Austin, TX: University of Texas Press.

United States Court of Appeals, Tenth Circuit. (September 20, 2004). D.C. No. 99-CV-0031-J. FindLaw for Legal Professionals. Retrieved from http://caselaw.lp.findlaw.com/cgi-bin/getcase.pl?court=10th&navby=ca. Accessed on October 4, 2007.

17

The Trees are Breathing Us: An Indigenous View of Relationship in Nature and Business

Kaylynn Sullivan TwoTrees and Matthew Kolan

Opening

Entering school was my initiation into mainstream American culture, and whenever I came home to my grandmother with questions from life outside her cabin she would pause for a moment and say "In the beginning was Great Mystery and from Great Mystery all things are born." It frustrated me at first, and then, as I grew older and traveled away from home, I forgot about it. Later, I found myself repeating it when my children were young, and I relied on it when I started teaching and working as an organizational consultant. Those words could shift my orientation back to the Earth and my grandmother's embodied understanding of Relationship.

When I said it myself as an adult, it felt like reaching back through time/space/ancestors/land for the oldest memory — the memory of being connected to all things and bringing that memory to life again. When my grandmother said it, she would stop for a few moments and then point to our relatives that she could see in the moment — the trees, the stones, the plants, the buffalo, fire, wind, water. She would remember all life on the earth. Her sense of Relationship crossed all borders and boundaries. It encompassed contradiction and opposition.

When most people use the word relationship, they seem focused on human relationships — our connection to each other. And this connection is often centered on similarities and compatibility. Yet the challenges of our age are firmly rooted in incommensurability — places where core values and beliefs are fundamentally different.

Using my grandmother's response still sends me back to a place that is large enough and mysterious enough to hold the tension of opposition within the same breath without creating separation. This is not something I understand, but I know when it is present as I listen to someone or something that contradicts my core values or beliefs. This feeling allows me to stop and listen for the birdsong or sound of wind and changes of light. It infuses my immediate impulse to contradict or advocate for my own position with spaciousness to listen. It gives me time to critically assess the larger patterns at play in the situation and to ask: What are the natural, societal, historical, and personal dynamics (seasons, weather, climate change, and dynamics of power and privilege) that are influencing the current moment?

This invites the possibility to engage with tension as a generative resource for creativity and innovation in service to life on the planet. Tension is often underutilized and not all expressions of tension lead to conflict. If we can discern the difference between tension that can burst open the seed coats of creativity and tension that leads to conflict and potential harm we can unlock much more of the creative potential of inherent differences and incommensurability in relationships.

My grandmother helped me to recognize that Relationship is always at the core. It includes the earth, the stones, the trees, the plants, the animals, all of nature, and humans as a part of the Whole. Seeing the human relationship as a part of a whole set of relationships that are nourished by the natural world, that keeps me connected to Mystery. When I focus only on the human in a relationship, I actually diminish my capacity for creativity.

Relationship is more important than profit, benefit, and even more important than understanding and happiness. Holding relationship at the core allows me to engage with every interaction realizing that I am learning and growing as part of something larger than ourselves.

This practice gives me a place to stand as a *maka wicasa*, an earth person, in Relationship with all of life stretching all the way back to Great Mystery. It reorients me to the Earth as mother/teacher/nourishment/medicine and to humans as one part of that large web of Relationship. It is from this foundation of Relationship that I can participate with the land, seasons, weather, gardens, wild spaces, birds and ground animals, insects, and humans in a dynamic balance of giving and receiving. And from that starting point I participate in business partnerships and collaborations that align with and grow from an understanding that we're part of a Whole. It allows me to engage with issues not as separate problems but rather as a way of continuing to enliven my Relationship with nature as collaborator, teacher, and partner.

For modern business practices to be built around having relational practices rather than transactional practices is key to working in an ethical, upright manner. It creates organizational cultures that embody these principles as a way to build relationship. With this core, both in leadership and the way organizations understand themselves as a culture, what happens in our business life becomes much more relevant to our living, and it transforms how we think of success.

The challenge remains that relationships are messy, and take time to build. The investment and up-front time needed to build the foundations of relationship are quite high. For that reason, many businesses have struggled to move beyond transactional business practices to relationship-centered practices. However, those businesses that do invest the time into Relationship often find that working together to reach goals and objectives is faster, more creative, and effective, because they're not making mistakes and dealing with misunderstandings that need to be cleaned up later.

It Takes Two to Know One

An embodied example of life/work relationship that both models and employs many of the principles discussed here is that of myself and Matt Kolan, my consulting and teaching colleague and friend. From this point on in this chapter everything here is written collaboratively with Matt. We rely on and utilize our relationship as the foundation of our work in the world. We continue to learn from each other what it means to live and work from a core of integrity while engaging as consultants/catalysts with individuals, organizations, and community groups. Relationship is the core of what we bring to our decade of work with environmental, environmental education, and social change organizations across the country.

Our personal and professional relationship began 10 years ago when we were both invited to cofacilitate a week-long retreat designed to strengthen relationships among environmental and social justice leaders from around the country. The retreat was intended to engage with contentious issues (race, class, power, and privilege) and required a facilitation team that was united and coherent. We first met in person about 3 hours before the retreat participants arrived and the retreat began. It was immediately clear that we were different. Really different. At a glance:

- At 6'6", Matt stands a full 1.5 feet taller than Kaylynn.
- Kaylynn is more than twice Matt's age.
- Matt is White. Kaylynn is brown.

- Kaylynn is firmly rooted in her Indigenous mind and cultural lineage, while Matt is deeply influenced by 23 years of formalized Western education.
- Matt was raised by middle-class parents. Kaylynn grew up knowing poverty.

We could go on. Given these differences, it seemed unfathomable that a few years later, after spending significant time and energy deepening our relationship, people would periodically meet us and think that we were relatives.

Yet in the first 15 minutes of our relationship, we also discovered parallels in our fundamental orientations. We are both committed to well-being for all life, remembering ourselves as part of something larger, an openness to learning and change, and following our Calling in the world. Yet it is worth noting, that our relationship didn't grow by just focusing on our similarities. The biggest source of growth has been our differences.

When introducing ourselves to each other, Matt mentioned that he was a tracker. "Interesting," Kaylynn noted, "I'm a tracker too. What do you track?" she asked him. Matt had never been asked this question before and noted that he tracks animals — foxes, bobcats, weasels, deer. He paused for a moment and then returned the question: "What do you track?" Kaylynn smiled, "Energy patterns and flows," she said.

Despite the obvious dissimilarities, this was perhaps our most fundamental difference — our unique ways of knowing and the divergent lenses through which we view the world. Many conversations and shared experiences followed over the years as we explored the differences in the ways we track. It has been these differences (probably more than our similarities) that have been such a rich source of generative tension and growth in our relationship.

We look to our relationship and its continued growth as the foundation of how we work together as collaborators with organizations and community groups. Over the last decade, we have established a series of practices, principles, and working agreements that help our relationship evolve while working to establish a Relationship-centered approach to doing work in the world.

Working Agreements

Over the years as our relationship has deepened, we have identified and articulated agreements that allow us to show up fully in our work together. These agreements are fluid and dynamic. We revisit them when our needs change or when one of us recognizes a pattern that isn't working.

The agreements and practices below offer a window into the process by which we have built our relationship together and how we relate to the natural world around us. They are also the practices we utilize to strengthen relationships with the organizational communities with which we work. We don't think of our partners as "clients" or organizations. Every organization is made up of people, and the first step in doing good work together is a process that creates the conditions for our collective relationships to flourish while illuminating the larger network of relationships, both human and nonhuman, that sustain each of us.

Showing up Ready

The first commitment that allows us to focus on relationship is rooted in our ongoing efforts to show up ready and enter our relationship upright. This doesn't mean that we are perfect or that we don't wobble. It doesn't mean that we don't have personal needs/wants, or that external circumstances don't impact us. But it does mean that we don't look to each other as the source of our individual well-being. Whenever possible, the focus of our connection is on the relationship itself, not what either of us might "get out of it." We have our own practices for getting clean, clear, centered, grounded, and connected. It's from this place that we are able to connect more fully and allow our relationship to be of service to our larger work.

Strength to Strength

In the same way that Kaylynn's grandmother's words remain an essential re-orientation, so have the teachings of her uncle who taught that meeting people "eye to eye and strength to strength" brought strength and well-being to our relationships. Meeting and working strength to strength does not mean that we are equal. We each have a variety of different gifts, skills, and experiences that we bring to our relationship. As we recognize these differences, it makes it possible for us to discern how our individual strengths can combine in synergistic ways and our collective efforts can best honor and make good use of those strengths. This requires a good deal of self-awareness (knowing our strengths and each other's strengths) and a clear sense of a shared purpose.

Risk to Gain

In order to work together to reach goals and objectives based on strong relationships it is essential to understand that each of us must be ready and willing to take risks. Most of us will take a risk in an attempt to avoid loss. In building organizational cultures based on strong relationships we must begin to develop the individual and collective capacity to risk in order to gain deeper and stronger connections. We can begin with very low risk experiences. This might mean being vulnerable or sharing more of our self with colleagues. For us, this low risk period began with sharing lots of personal stories and experiences in order to have a fuller picture of each other and discover new strengths. As the foundation of the relationship deepened, we shared more moments of discomfort/ disagreement/discord in expressing our differences.

There have been many moments along the way when we recognized the opportunity to go deeper and broader with each other. These moments are filled with questions:

"What will they think of me?"

"Is this going too far across the line?"

"Will they be able to handle it?"

In spite of these questions, we have found it worthwhile to take risks to grow the foundation of the relationship. It is the continual process of sharing stories and taking progressively deeper risks that have created the groundwork to be able to engage with complex and difficult conversations. Some of the moments of greater risk have occurred when talking about colonization and the appropriation that is possible when working at the crossroads of Western and Indigenous knowledge. It also created a foundation where we could consciously work to alter/interrupt the historical transactional and colonial patterns that have appropriated Indigenous knowledge as we built our joint capacity to discern when these patterns may arise. These experiences have increased our awareness and ability to engage with and address these issues when they come up in our work with organizations and community groups.

Capital "T" Trust

Trust is often cited as one of the most fundamental qualities of a healthy relationship. Trust is often used as a measure of reliability and consistency (e.g., We can trust Mike because he does what he says he will do). This type of trust creates a sense of security that comes from being able to rely on the consistent behavior of others. Yet this kind of trust doesn't account for the fact that people are dynamic and constantly changing. If our relationships are built on trust rooted in reliability, we may be unconsciously undermining each other's growth and evolution. In fact, we've seen many people deemed "untrustworthy" when they make unexpected choices that don't align with previous behaviors or when they go through significant transitions that change their way of showing up in the world.

During our work together we have been exploring an expression of trust that we call capital "T" Trust. This type of Trust has grown from our consistent and reliable commitment to relationship but is also rooted in our sense of ourselves as part of something larger, our openness to learning and change, and our commitment to our Calling in the world. Capital "T" Trust grows from a deep practice of prioritizing well-being; our own well-being, the well-being of each other, and the well-being of the larger World of which we are part. Occasionally, this results in behavior that can be perceived to others as unreliable as we make decisions that place well-being ahead of consistency.

Neither of us is particularly consistent. Yet, our relationship offers us the support and freedom to continually change and evolve. This expression of Trust has led us to many conversations about the nature of reciprocity in our relationship. And in the early days of working together, we carefully and intentionally tended to the quality of our relationship; making sure that it was "exothermic" (generating energy), building our capacity to engage in tension, aligning our strengths (rather than aligning one person's strengths with the other's weakness), being committed to fair (but not necessarily equal) exchange. And while this is still important, as our Trust for each other grew, our sense of reciprocity also shifted. Rather than being primarily concerned with the dynamic balance of our relationship/connection, we shifted our attention to exploring how our relationship might benefit and serve the larger World of which we are part.

Working/Living in Relationship

The agreements and practices described above are central to our relationship with each other as well as our capacity to work with our partner organizations and community groups. Our own use of these practices for over 10 years of working with environmental, educational, and social justice organizations has changed the way we do our work. In order to shift organizational change work from a historically transactional approach to a relational way of doing business, it has been necessary to create new measures of success that are focused on relationship. This means that our stated goal is not to make our partners or each other happy. It's about strengthening relationship — between us and the partners, inside the organization, and between the organization and its surrounding human and natural communities.

Although most of the organizations with whom we work identify the importance of relationship in their mission, vision, and values, it is often challenging to interrupt the embedded patterns of transactional engagement that show up in the daily operations and interactions. We have found the following set of practices to be deeply relational and have experienced the way they can interrupt transactional patterns at the daily operational level and also in terms of the larger strategic plans of an organization.

Nature is Our Nature

When we breathe we are *being* Nature. We are connected to the trees that are breathing us. It is not necessary to bring nature in or go out into nature, because we ARE nature. If we start there, then it gives us a different relationship to the green, to the trees, the grasses. This reminds us that we are details of the landscape, just like everything else.

This is a fundamental starting point when we work with organizations. To help us keep this orientation, we often use some of the basic principles of healthy natural systems — uniqueness, diversity, interdependence, self-organization, and emergence. These principles provide a learning arc for our work and help us discern appropriate practices to use in any given moment.

Non-Comparative Perception

One of the great challenges of listening is to be aware of the editing process that goes on internally. "Non-Comparative perception" brings awareness to our listening and processing and asks us to suspend comparison, scripting and connecting in order to allow for one's full presence in the activity of listening. It decentralizes the binary process of accept/reject thinking. In suspending comparison, we are asked to simply hear what is being said without comparing it immediately to our opinions and beliefs. This practice asks the listener to set aside their own ideology and become a detail of the listening rather than the center. This practice enhances our capacity to hear divergent ideas and perspectives without challenging our own identity or self-worth; creating the possibility for differentiated relationships to flourish.

Deep Listening, Talking Circle, and Dialogue

The practice of non-comparative perception is fundamental to our ability to listen deeply to each other and communicate consciously. While communication is a fundamental aspect of relationships, not all forms of conversation strengthen the quality of interpersonal relationships. In fact, many patterns of communication lead to disconnection. Most people have experience with conversations where being right, being heard, persuading others, and justifying assumptions are the norm. Whenever possible, we try to interrupt that dynamic by practicing modes of communication that emphasize learning and nurture relationship.

One expression of this is the Talking Circle or Circle Process. The term "talking circle" has been used to identify many forms of circular communication. If we go back to Kaylynn's grandmother's world, Circle Process realigns communication with nature by following rhythms and patterns of the sun or the moon. This creates space for a different kind of conversation. Circle Process invites us to listen and speak from a cyclical, relational way of knowing. Attention is paid to listening: to the voices of the participants, to the spaces between the voices, to the surrounding environment, and to the relationship of these things to one another and to the Whole. This process acknowledges the presence of people and world views not present or expressed as part of the Whole. This means more than trying to remember everyone you thought might be left out by adding another place in the circle. It is actually listening for what might be absent but unknown and making room for it to reveal itself.

Another communication practice that we use with our partnering organizations and communities is dialogue. We approach dialogue from our own unique perspective as a process for exploring new territory. The goal is not consensus or agreement. Rather the space is held to explore the tension of our differences and learn how our unique perspectives might generate and reveal new possibilities and insights. Dialogue focuses on group inquiry (not advocacy) and when it works well, it creates conditions for a group to discover insights that aren't attainable individually.

Dialogue process invites groups to engage curiosity, suspend judgment, examine blind spots, and listen for the larger wisdom that is present in the group.

Remembering

In over a decade of working together it has been essential for us to find a way to reorient ourselves towards Relationship. It is not my grandmother invoking "in the beginning was Great Mystery and out of Great Mystery all things are born" which realigns us in our work, although I have told the story to Matt many times and he occasionally uses that phrase with me. We continue to find new ways for that re-orientation to remain dynamic and embodied in our relationship with each other, the natural world around us and in our work. In every new situation with a community or organization we do this first by remembering gratitude for being a part of the trees that are breathing us and the Earth that shares her bounty with us. We remember that we are a detail of whatever landscape that we inhabit and begin our work from there.

Conclusion: Responses of the Non-indigenous Business World to Indigenous Initiatives

18

Weaving IWOK into the Storying of Business, Ethics, and the Busy-Ness of Being Human

Maria Humphries

One lives their living story in a web of living stories

— Boje (2001, 2008)

"Boozhoo!" ["Greetings!"] write Verbos, Kennedy, and Claw in the opening of Chapter 10. Their greeting is followed by a thoughtful introduction that gives insight into the relationships these women have with others and with Earth. Greetings are often the first visible sign of relationship. Relationship is the key concept through which the Eight Aspects of Tribal Wisdom connect (Aspects are listed by Grace Ann in Preface, pp. xiii-xiv and Ch. 1, p. 5). I resonate with the opening greeting in Chapter 10 and I follow this lead.

"Groetjes!" ["Greetings!"]. I am a woman of Dutch descent. I live and work in New Zealand — known also as Aotearoa. I am a grandmother, mother, sister, daughter, and friend. I am also a teacher and researcher with three decades of expressed interest in the organization and management of our humanity. My desire to provide a greeting as a making of a relationship with readers as

225

Amy has done is more fully explained in Humphries, Dey, and Casey-Cox (2016). There we show how indigenous ideas of greeting and relationship-making common in the communities I am familiar with has enriched my personal understanding of my relationship with the present, the past, and the future. This enrichment influences my understanding of the human relationship with the material and non-material world. Its relational emphasis is enhanced by the influence of Maori (the indigenous peoples of Aotearoa) that impact ways of being that in this jurisdiction extend into many educational practices and are filtering into social and economic policy and thus into business related protocols.

I have been a teacher and researcher in organizational studies for over twenty-five years. How and what management scholars might learn from indigenous people has been an abiding aspect of my work and can be seen for example in Humphries (1992), Humphries and Martin (2005), Fitzgibbons and Humphries (2011), Hoskins, Martin, and Humphries (2011), and Verbos and Humphries (2014). The invitation to contribute to a book with its emphasis on Native American Tribal Wisdom or IWOK has been accepted in all humility and recognition of my not being of that world. I accept the invitation with much gratitude for the many things I continue to learn in the doing and the becoming that this writing enables.

The work of many authors — indigenous and non-indigenous authorities — resonates for me in my abiding interest in the work of critical organizational theorists. These authors are concerned with the ever-deepening colonization of the life-world through the intensification of an economic instrumentalism being intensified the world over. This instrumentalism appears to be generated from a de-animated, de-spiritualized depiction of Earth. This depiction, taken as a guiding and constraining genesis story, continues to diminish our full humanity and intensifies the stress we place on Earth. The ever greater accessibility to indigenous ideas to a wider population invoke a more animated, spirit-filled ways to guide our thinking about ethics, sustainability, and responsibility — ideas not unknown to non-indigenous peoples but often subjugated to the economic order(s) increasingly difficult to locate in human decisions by their very embeddedness — hidden as they are in plain sight.

Threaded through this book is the significance of stories in learning what it is to lead a good and courageous life. We are encouraged to rethink our ways of being, and to revisit our ideas about our very identity as humans. We are not alone in this. The cosmos too has a voice. Earth provides teachings. All life is entangled energy and all living creatures — humans among them — are always in *affectual* relationships. We can read of the restating of European interest in the animated being of Earth in the words chosen by Pope Francis in his 2015 Encyclia on *Care for our Common Home*.[1] In this letter Pope Francis is addressing not only the world's estimated 1.2 billion Catholics — but all people with a spiritual orientation. His animation of Earth is given a form as a living relation — a sister. He writes:

1. *"LAUDATO SI', mi' Signore"* — *"Praise be to you, my Lord"*. In the words of this beautiful canticle, Saint Francis of Assisi reminds us that our common home is like a sister with whom we share our life and a beautiful mother who opens her arms to embrace us. "Praise be to you, my Lord, through our Sister, Mother Earth, who sustains and governs us, and who produces various fruit with coloured flowers and herbs."[1]

2. This sister now cries out to us because of the harm we have inflicted on her by our irresponsible use and abuse of the goods with which God has endowed her. We have come to see ourselves as her lords and masters, entitled to plunder her at will. The violence present in our hearts, wounded by sin, is also reflected in the symptoms of sickness evident in the soil, in the water, in the air and in all forms of life. This is why the earth herself, burdened and laid waste, is among the most abandoned and maltreated of our poor; she "groans

---

1. https://laudatosi.com/watch

in travail" (*Rom* 8:22). We have forgotten that we ourselves are dust of the earth (cf. *Gen* 2:7); our very bodies are made up of her elements, we breathe her air and we receive life and refreshment from her waters.

We each live in specific time and place. We each have a capacity and a responsibility to respond to the "harm we have inflicted" on Earth and her many creatures — including our fellow human beings. This orientation draws us to an ethics "answerability" prioritized in this book.

Changing by Being Differently in the World

Gregory Cajete invites us to understand how indigenous stories "relate the experience of life lived in time and place" (2015, p. 96). He writes that we humans are "storied and storying beings" and it's time to change the "story line"; "changing story lines of dysfunctional to ones of functionality, moving towards health" (*ibid.*). Indigenous stories he writes "have deep roots" in the very "heart of the human psyche" and "the geography of the human soul" (p. 96). A focus on storying is an approach to attending to desirable transformation in the ways we are human that is gathering pace and influence in the Academy. It is an approach to understanding and acting in the world. It is a way to think about how and why we may wish to influence change in the trajectory of our humanity and our relationship with planet earth. It is a way of encouraging wisdom in our actions. It is a call to notice our storying that can be seen very explicitly in the call to transform our way of being human in the drumming of the International Council of Thirteen Grandmothers[2] and in a call by Korten (2015) to change the future by changing the story by which we will create that future.

"But" I hear many of my peers and students say with skepticism and often impatience, "just changing a story will not change

---

2. http://www.grandmotherscouncil.org/

the terrible things going on in the world." And many times I feel this way too. Yet — I know from experience that as I change the stories I choose to listen to, the stories I tell myself, the stories I write, the stories I choose to tell — and where and how I tell them, I am changing. And as I notice I am changing so too I know we can change the way we are human — the way we "story our being in the world" (Boje, 2014). Finding ways to learn from indigenous wisdoms has been a significant part of my experience.

Why am I Drawn to Indigenous Storying?

Critical Management Studies (CMS) takes as its starting point a mandate to expose to view systemic exploitations and degradations with an intent to change these towards ways of being human that are more equitable, more life enhancing, and urgently restorative of Earth. This mandate has always attracted my attention and much energy — but has also been limited in the opportunity to express the full scope of my concerns and interests. What seemed missing for me in much of the CMS genre is its lack of recognition of a generous, generative, and emancipatory spiritual dynamics. CMS however, came closest to a secularized form of liberation theology through which I could channel my energies and attention in a career as a business school teacher and researcher. An enduring thread of my work has been to stay focused on *why* my attraction to the increasingly assertive voices of indigenous people seemed to hold my attention. The stories of *why* is complex. Initially I was moved by the stories about the undeniable observation that the indigenous people in my world were overly represented in negative social statistics of all kinds. I wanted to be part of "fixing" this. I had much to learn! I have needed to shift my story about myself from "I want to help" to trying to understand much more profoundly how I am part of the story that gives the outcomes I am concerned about. This realization gave much pertinence to Gandhi's "be the change in the world." This dawning was galvanized in coming across a call by Lilla Watson, Gangulu woman and Muri visual artist with which this book is opened. It is worth repeating. Watson writes

> If you have come here to help me, you are wasting our time. But if you have come, because your liberation is tied up with mine, then let us work together.

This call has remained with me in all manner of concerns about justice, well-being, and in my professional context — work associated with organizational development. It has drawn me to the restoring of the relationship that is necessary not only between indigenous and non-indigenous peoples but also in seeking to understand the many ways our fates are entangled.

Change is Inevitable, Change is Necessary — but from What to What?

In contributing to a book about IWOK and tribal wisdom, it is pertinent to emphasize I am not an indigenous person in the various ways this is defined by indigenous peoples themselves, or the legalistic definitions driving neo-colonial policy and practice. How is it that I, in my capacity as a management educator, mother, daughter, citizen, might draw on indigenous wisdom, when I am not steeped in the traditions of a tribe that gives embodiment and meaning to a set of values? How can the call to this idea of answerability manifest in my life? What can I learn from the increasing visibility of indigenous wisdom? How can I discern what is an ethical reference to indigenous values in a way of the world that from a CMS perspective, ultimately seeks to absorb all potential ways of being to system-preserving adaptations.

I have been drawn to the work of David Boje for over twenty years. David is unafraid to cause disruption to the patterning of our thoughts and ways of being. Disruption is necessary — and we need not fear it. Disruption in my early view of indigenous people as in need of my help in the face of so many challenges brought about by the processes of colonization was a step towards a different way of being. IWOK has brought me to a different orientation to answerability. What does it mean to be answerable to the situation we humans have brought ourselves to? And who or what are we answerable to? In the disruption of exploitative human practices, how can aspects of indigenous wisdom generate change in who I am, how I story my life and thus how I contribute to the invigoration of justice broadly conceived as a universal expression of an ethics that endorses the flourishing of life? Is there a voice I can project that is not the voice of missionary, of helper, of rescuer and thus the neo-colonial arrogance I now sense in these forms of seeking to help, manage, change? I take heart from the story told by TwoTrees and Kolan in Chapter 17. I am always in relation — and I have much to learn. I need courage to ensure I do not fear disruption to my way of knowing anything at any time. I am encouraged by their reminder that we humans "are a detail of whatever landscape that we inhabit" and we can begin our work from there — each day anew.

In What Ways Can I be Part of the Re-storying of Humanity?

There are many ways we can re-story our human future that together will bring the material and spiritual changes I so much desire to see in the world. The authors contributing to this book give me many ways to expand my thinking, my sense of self, my sense of answerability to the enhancement not degradation of life — and in so doing to change the way I am in the world. It is a form of change infused by the relational ethics so articulately expressed by the various authors who have contributed to this book. The values expressed in IWOK as depicted in this book, are not unique to North American indigenous expressions. They reverberate in the region of Mother Earth where I live and work. They pulse in the relationships with Earth we might deepen if when we see ourselves as entangled always in spiritual and material ways with all that is life. With Grace Ann I proffer that finding resonances between tribal wisdoms and Euro-Western scholarship may guide us to a bridge between these different ways of being. While we can never fully understand another's experience except in a mediated, approximate way we can aspire to a greater respect and connection. We can work to be cautious about the risks of *discoverers* who may select only those "parts of indigenous knowledge that fit with their imperialistic viewpoints" as Pepion cautions us in Chapter 2. If we take the thoughts in this book as gifts — gifts that encourage us to consider IWOK in our thinking, writing, and being — we may have some guideposts to give us glimmers of our goal of better understanding each of the other. As we are able to experience the other, we may see and understand ourselves better in the gift of mutuality. From such a position, we will have greater potential for mutual influence through a cocreated story for the thriving of life in a world worth working for.

References

Boje, D. M. (2001). *Narrative methods for organizational and communication research*. London: Sage.

Boje, D. M. (2008). *Storytelling organizations*. London: Sage.

Boje, D. M. (2014). *Storytelling organizational practices: Managing in the quantum age*. London: Routledge.

Cajete, G. A. (2015). *Indigenous community: Rekindling the teachings of the seventh fire*. St. Paul, MN: Living Justice Press.

Fitzgibbons, D. E., & Humphries, M. T. Guest Co-Editor (2011). Enhancing the circle of life: Management education and Indigenous Knowledge. *Journal of Management Education*, February 2011, *35*(1), 3–7.

Hoskins, T. K., Martin, B., & Humphries, M. T. (2011). The power of relational responsibility. EJBO — Electronic Journal of Business Ethics and Organization Studies, *16*(2), 22–27.

Humphries, M. T. (1992). Working with our differences: New Zealand experiences. *Journal of Management Education*, *16*(Suppl. 4), 28–42.

Humphries, M. T., Dey, K. J., & Casey-Cox, A. (2016). Shopping consciously! Putting theory into educational practice: Re-storying the need for plastic. In S. Roz & J. Leigh (Eds.), Leadership and the PRME. Sheffield, UK: Greenleaf Publishing.

Humphries, M. T., & Martin, B. (2005). Diversity ethics: A compass pointing to relationality and responsibility for navigating turbulent seas. *International Journal of Knowledge, Culture and Change Management*, *4*, 1235–1240.

Korten, D. (2015). *Change the story, change the future*. Oakland, CA: Berrett-Koehler.

Verbos, A., & Humphries, M. T. (2014). A native American relational ethic: An indigenous perspective on teaching human responsibility. *Journal of Business Ethics*, 123(1), 1–9.

Tribal Wisdom in Today's Business Environment

19

Grace Ann Rosile

The Eight Aspects of Tribal Wisdom, introduced in the Preface, have examples woven throughout this book. Below are the Eight Aspects, followed by selected business examples which have appeared in various parts of this book.

Eight Aspects of Tribal Wisdom	
1. *Relationships*	are an end in themselves
2. *Gifting*	is valued more highly
3. *Egalitarianism*	is preferred
4. *Non-Acquisitiveness*	is valued not greed
5. *Usefulness*	or access to use is valued
6. *Barter*	for what is needed
7. *Trust*	and Buyer Trust are valued
8. *Disclosure*	is full and voluntary

UNIVERSITY OF WINCHESTER
LIBRARY

1. **Relationships:** Mr. Jerry Smith of the Laguna Development Corporation retains his casino executives more than three times longer than the average industry tenure. As part of his emphasis on relationships rooted in respect and trust, he likes to promote from within. Also, he assures his executives that they will not be ousted from their jobs by sometimes-tumultuous tribal politics. Another example of valuing relationships is the case of Acoma Pueblo, where Mary Tenorio worked within the traditional leadership structure of her tribe, maintaining good relationships while introducing economically beneficial changes. In both cases, good relationships were also good for business.

2. **Gifting:** Gift-giving philosophy includes the commonly popular free samples, but also goes beyond that. Dr. Joe Gladstone's research documents an American Indian restaurant owner whose philosophy is that he gives his very best to his customers. He goes beyond the minimum acceptable, because he views his product as more than an exchange for money. His product is a reflection of himself. He views his product as a gift of the best that he can offer.

3. **Egalitarianism:** Verbos, Kennedy, and Claw recount the experience of Cherokee Chief Chad "Corntassel" Smith as he observes an old man working in a Goodwill store. Smith's story reminds us of each person's value, reflecting appreciation for them as well as humility that we are not better than others.

4. **Non-Acquisitiveness:** The Winnebago Tribe's Ho Chunk, Inc., helps tribal people with down payments on housing, and with fair terms on used cars through Rez Cars. Rather than greedily seeking higher profits for the company in areas where other providers are scarce, instead, this company helps tribal people obtain needed housing and transportation at reasonable prices. (See Verbos, Kennedy, and Claw in Chapter 10.)

5. **Usefulness:** We see usefulness as a main consideration in Stewart and Pascal's case exercise of deciding whether to locate a business near its tribal home or near larger

population centers. Profit alone is not the only consideration. Usefulness, or value to the tribe, is a more complex benefit, which is sometimes less easily measured than monetary profit.

6. **Barter:** Sanchez discusses how NOVA Corporation barters by taking student interns. The company offers expertise in the form of learning experiences for student interns. The students offer energy, fresh perspectives, and a sort of almost-free trial period of work. Typically this gives the company an advantage in identifying, trying out, and hiring the best of the student interns. Equally, internship experience is quite valuable on the resume of an otherwise-inexperienced graduate.

7. **Trust:** Verbos, Kennedy, and Claw provide the case example of Mno-Bmadsen's CEO Mr. Troyland Clay. Clay's endorsement of the Seven Grandfather teachings extends not only to his own companies, but also to all with whom they do business. By following the teachings (which include honesty and truth), and by refusing to do business with those who do not demonstrate the same ethical standards, they build trusting business relationships.

8. **Disclosure:** Boardman discusses the historical norms among indigenous peoples for full and honest disclosure in trading activities. TwoTrees and Kolan translate that social norm into ways to enhance work relationships, ways which extend from interpersonal to social to humanity's relationship with nature. Using non-comparative listening allows both listeners and tellers to be open about their differences, and to enjoy creative tension as a positive experience that can strengthen relationships. Using TwoTrees and Kolan's various methods of speaking and listening creates the safe nurturing environment where personal risks and disclosure is welcome, productive, and relationship-enhancing.

Epilogue: What Does It Mean?

I want to end by circling back to where we started, back to Fixico's report of Russell Means' grandfather story.

Fixico (2003) quotes noted Indian activist Russell Means (who we are sad to say died in 2012):

> Grandpa John told me endless stories about young men who had opportunities to live up to their names. One day, he said, "there was a young man named Looks Twice — really, he was more like a boy — who left his village alone to hunt, hoping to bring back some meat. He wanted to prove that he was a man. It was in the springtime. He went without a bow or a lance, and he killed a deer with his knife"...."How did he kill the deer, Grandpa?" I interrupted. "You'd better figure that out," he said. "That's what will make you a man" (Fixico, 2003, p. 88). (See p. 90 in this volume)

Recall that we began this book with the statement: **Wisdom must be sought, not taught**.

What wisdom do we find in this story? To assist those of us not brought up in the kind of context where clues to the meaning of the story would be found if one sought them, we offer some suggestions.

First, we consider the detail that the young brave Looks Twice had an opportunity to live up to his name. What does that mean? Perhaps it means he had an opportunity to look twice, but what was he supposed to be looking at? Let's look further into the story.

In the story, we see that Looks Twice killed a deer without his bow or lance, only with his knife. If you have had the opportunity to see deer in the forest, as I used to do when I went riding though acres of Pennsylvania woodlands, you would know that deer are pretty shy and spooky. When they saw me, they would freeze for a moment, then bound off in an instant. Note here that there is a reason behind the old saying that someone "runs like a deer." Deer are very quick and fast. The ones who venture into suburban neighborhoods have become accustomed to people, and will linger over a tasty shrub much longer than deer in the wild.

So we see that in the wild, it is very difficult to get close to a deer. Therefore, in previous times, a bow or lance would be used to cover the greater distances. Although I am no expert, I have seen (again when riding in the woods) hunters camouflaged in a tree, waiting near a deer trail for the deer to pass by close enough for their bows to find their targets.

How could Looks Twice get close enough to kill a deer with his knife? Here I think of the old saying, "If something looks too good to be true, it probably is (false)." Perhaps this was when Looks Twice should have looked again. Instead, he killed the deer with his knife.

The story tells us it was in the springtime. What happens in the spring? Deer give birth to their young. Could the deer have been in labor? Or could the deer have been old and ill? There must have been some unusual reason for the brave to be able to get so close. If our young brave had looked again, he might have discovered the reason.

Means (in Fixico 2003) reports further details of his grandfather's story, involving heavy spring rains and a flooded stream. When Means asks his grandfather whether the young brave crossed the stream, returned home, and became a man, his grandfather says "You figure it out" (Fixico 2003, p. 89). To find out what Means learned, the reader is referred to Means with Wolf 1995, p. 18, or Fixico 2003, pp. 88-89. Our purpose here is not to discover someone else's meaning. Rather, this story is repeated to invite you, the reader, to find your own meaning in it.

The young Looks Twice did not look twice. And since he had gone hunting alone, there were no other braves with him who might have seen what he must have missed. We do not know the traditions of this particular tribe, but for many tribes, Rosile, Pepion, and Gladstone (2012) notes that it was forbidden to hunt alone. There were probably reasons of efficiency for such a rule, and also, strategic sustainability-related reasons. The tribe would not want to over-kill and endanger the survival of the entire herd. Instead, they might plan how and when to harvest a scarce resource like deer.

A tribe might also, as a group, decide how to distribute the bounty from hunting. Here again, Rosile et al. (2012) notes that the elders might be given the first portions of food from a hunt. Such difficult choices might not always be free from controversy. However, these kinds of choices routinely arose in tribal cultures.

For details about making such choices, the reader is encouraged to discover the wonderful classic small book "Two Old Women: An Alaska Legend of Betrayal, Courage, and Survival" by Velma Wallis (1993). The book jacket describes this story as follows:

> Based on an Athabaskan Indian legend passed along from mothers to daughters for many generations on the upper Yukon River in Alaska, this is the tragic and shocking story — with a surprise ending — of two elderly women abandoned by a migrating tribe that faces starvation brought on by unusually harsh Arctic weather and a shortage of fish and game.

This story of "Two Old Women" demonstrates the importance of survival of the tribe, even if it might mean the abandonment of some individuals. Some perspectives on Euro-Western ethics call this the "greatest good for the greatest number." A virtue-ethics approach might suggest the value of sharing with others.

The Kantian rules-based view of ethics would suggest we should follow the rules our societies have established. For indigenous ethics, relationships are of primary importance.

Regarding Russell Means' grandfather's story, for our young brave Looks Twice, it might not have been in the interest of the tribe for an individual to hunt alone for his family. Sometimes rugged individualism may work to the detriment of the group. In systems theory terms, it is widely accepted that some sub-systems must operate at sub-optimal level for the entire system to achieve optimum performance.

The ethical dilemma remains: How do we know when to take initiative as an individual, and when to "look twice" and consider the group? Both are good, but not always at the same times. Because both are good actions in themselves, we have difficulty choosing which "good" is "best" in a given situation, hence the dilemma.

Ethical dilemmas abound in life. Most cultures have short-hand stories used to convey moral advice. Sometimes we call these "aphorisms" or in the Hispanic culture "dichos" (sayings) to guide our actions. However, for every saying there is usually an opposite one. So, for example, "You snooze, you lose" means don't move too slowly. And "Look before you leap" means don't move too quickly. The dilemma is in choosing which good action will result in the best outcome in a particular situation. Wisdom means being able to decide which advice to follow in the midst of messy real-life experiences.

Like anything else, practice helps. Cajete talks of building "story muscles." In lieu of actual experience, one of the best ways to practice making choices is through stories. Stories allow us to vicariously experience the outcomes of various decisions in life-like situations. We can learn to make better, more ethical choices by observing the outcomes of choices made by characters in our stories.

Let us return to Looks Twice. What lessons were in his story? We find at least six.

1. When something seems too good to be true, look again, because it may not be so good.

2. What appears good to the individual, may not always be good for the group.

3. Traditions (like the taboo on hunting alone) are there for a reason, and based on the wisdom of our elders. Do not discard them lightly.

4. Consider the long-term as well as the short-term effects of your actions (sustainability).

5. Looks Twice, already described as young and more of a boy than a man, wanted to prove he was a man. Some would say that a man would have no need of proving anything.

6. Finally, understand the context. What works in one situation may not work in another. The best way to learn such lessons is through experience, whether first hand or through stories. Then we can take from such experiences the desire to look twice, to reflect on our own decision-making processes and understanding of the situation.

Wisdom comes from the self-awareness of who I am and in what context I find myself. If "The early bird gets the worm," am I the bird or the worm? Or some other being? As Steven Wright has said: "The early bird gets the worm, but the second mouse gets the cheese." In short, we learn how to seek wisdom as we make those difficult choices in life about what advice to follow, and sometimes, the choice is about following no advice except our own inner voice. Wisdom cannot be taught, because I cannot fully know your unique context. Wisdom can be, and must be, sought by each individual for themselves. We hope this volume provides assistance in that search.

Grace Ann Rosile
Editor

References

Fixico, D. (2003). *The American Indian mind in a linear world: American Indian studies & traditional knowledge*. London: Routledge.

Means, R., & Wolf, M. J. (1995). *Where white men fear to tread: The autobiography of Russell means*. New York, NY: St. Martin's Press.

Rosile, G. A., Pepion, D., & Gladstone, J. (2012). Daniels principles of business ethics and tribal ethics: Using indigenous methods of storytelling to convey moral principles. In January 2012 DFEI conference presentation, Hotel Encanto, Las Cruces, NM.

Wallis, V. (1993). *Two old women: An Alaskan legend of betrayal, courage, and survival*. Harper Collins.

About the Authors

Calvin M. Boardman is Professor Emeritus of Finance at the David Eccles School of Business, University of Utah. He worked in the private sector for a variety of companies and taught for universities in the United States and around the world. He has published journal articles in finance and ethics and two books on the philosophy of business. He has been a board member of many profit and nonprofit organizations, among which was the Indian Walk-in Center in Salt Lake City. He has focused over 15 years on the study of trading philosophy worldwide but particularly on early Native American trade.

David M. Boje <www.davidboje.com> is Regents Professor of Management at New Mexico State University. He is an international and highly esteemed scholar in the areas of storytelling and antenarratives in organizations. He also holds an honorary doctorate from Aalborg University, and is considered godfather of their Material Storytelling Lab. He is founder of *Tamara Journal of Critical Organization Inquiry*. He has published 21 books, including *Storytelling Organizational Practices: Managing in the quantum age* (Routledge, 2014). His 141 journal articles have appeared in top-tier journals such as *Management Science, Administrative Science Quarterly, Organization Studies, Human Relations, and Academy of Management Journal*.

Gregory Cajete is Tewa Indian from Santa Clara Pueblo, New Mexico, whose work is dedicated to honoring the foundations of indigenous knowledge in education. Dr. Cajete has served as Dean of the Center for Research and Cultural Exchange, Chair of Native American Studies and Professor of ethno-science, at the Institute of American Indian Arts in Santa Fe, New Mexico. Currently, he is Director of Native American Studies and a Professor in the Division of Language, Literacy and Socio Cultural Studies in the College of Education at the University of New Mexico. Dr. Cajete has authored seven books, 22 book chapters, numerous articles, and over 250 national and international presentations.

Carma M. Claw is second year doctoral student at New Mexico State University. Her research interests include indigenous business management, ethics, and strategy. She offers over 17 years of industry experience, and has a commitment to Native American communities. Carma is Bit'ahnii and born for Kinlichii'nii, and a citizen of the Diné Nation.

Lisa Grayshield is member of the Washoe Tribe of Nevada and California. She is Associate Professor of Counseling and Educational Psychology at New Mexico State University. Dr. Grayshield's research interests include Indigenous Ways of Knowing (IWOK) in counseling and psychology. Specifically, she is interested in the incorporation of Indigenous knowledge forms as viable options for the way counseling and psychology is conceptualized, taught, practiced, and researched. Dr. Grayshield has been active as a board member for the NMSU Teaching Academy. She also served as the VP of the Native Concerns Group for the American Multicultural Counseling Division (AMCD).

Maria Humphries is Associate Professor at the Waikato Management School of the University of Waikato in Hamilton, New Zealand. How non-indigenous people might respond to the increasing accessibility of aspects of indigenous wisdom has been an enduring thread to her critical concern with the management of diversity for over 25 years. She sees in this emergent visibility, many opportunities for mutual attention to the significant indivisible environmental, social, political, and economic issues facing humanity. She is working with Professor David Boje and colleagues to explore the extent to which Hegelian Dialectics could be employed to serve the necessary transformation of our ways of being human and our relationship with Earth.

Deanna M. Kennedy, Ph.D., is Assistant Professor at the University of Washington Bothell. She is a member of the Cherokee Nation of Oklahoma. She is a proponent of Native student college preparation activities including Reaching American Indian Nations (R.A.I.N) and the Tribal Education Network (T-E-N).

Matthew Kolan is an avid naturalist and tracker. He is inspired by the wisdom of nature and the language of the land. Matt directs the University of Vermont's Leadership for Sustainability Masters Program, and teaches courses on the ecology of leadership; power and privilege; and field ecology. His research explores leadership and learning practices that are attuned to ecological principles and challenge colonial patterns of power/privilege that are perpetuated in many change-making initiatives. Matt also works as a consultant for a variety of organizations, helping build capacity for organizational learning and working with difference and tension in a generative way.

Gerri Elise McCulloh, Ph.D., teaches at New Mexico State University. Her research refocused the ancient philosophy of Pythagoras, feminist materialism, and the biological communication of a living planet, shifting emphasis away from linear designs of meaning toward nonlinear impressions, invitations, and invocations in acoustic rhetoric, requiring intra-active listening skills. Sounds and soundscapes, coupled with her love of language and stories, framed her early understandings, eventually inspiring her career as a broadcast journalist in community radio, news, and audio production. McCulloh is an activist, public speaker, and writer, teaching Rhetoric, Business composition, Technical and Scientific Communication, Documentary Film, and Environmental Discourse.

Vincent J. Pascal is Professor of Marketing at Eastern Washington University. He received his Ph.D. in Marketing from Washington State University, MBA from Gonzaga University, and BS from the United States Military Academy. He has published in the *Journal of Advertising, Journal of Consumer Issues and Research in Advertising,*

Journal of Research in Marketing and Entrepreneurship, *Journal of Strategic Marketing*, *Journal of Internet Commerce*, *Journal of International Marketing Strategy*, *International Journal of Innovation and Entrepreneurship*, to name a few. He is a recent chair for the American Marketing Association's Special Interest Group on Entrepreneurial Marketing and a Kauffman Grant recipient.

Donald D. Pepion, EdD, is College Professor who teaches Native American Studies courses in the Anthropology Department at New Mexico State University. Pepion has an extensive background in education, health, and tribal government including an appointment as President of Blackfeet Community College. As an enrolled member of the Blackfeet Indian Nation, he is a member of the following societies: Brave Dog, Rough Riders, Medicine Pipe, and Beaver Bundle. The elders of the Blackfeet Nation honored him as a leader in a War-bonnet transfer ceremony in 1985.

Grace Ann Rosile, Ph.D. <garosile@nmsu.edu> is Professor of Management at New Mexico State University. Her research interests include ethics, narrative, indigenous storytelling, restorying, and Ensemble Leadership. She has published numerous articles in over a dozen academic journals, and many book chapters. As an NMSU Daniels Fund Ethics Fellow for 5 years, Rosile produced and co-wrote a series of seven films on "Tribal Wisdom for Business Ethics," available at http://business.nmsu.edu/research/programs/daniels-ethics/tribal-ethics/. She is also founder of HorseSense at Work, using restorying, embodied storytelling, and equine-assisted storytelling for enhancing leadership, teamwork, and communication with work teams, families, and military veterans (www.horsesenseatwork.com).

Mabel Sanchez has a B.A. (magna cum laude) in International Business and an M.B.A. from the University of Texas at El Paso. She is currently a Ph.D. student at New Mexico State University. Mabel has lived in Mexico, United States, France, and London. Experiencing the different cultures has marked her research interest in diversity, gender and organization, alternative paradigms, organizational change, feminist theory, and qualitative research.

Mabel came back to the United States-Mexico borderland to study diversity, where one finds a mélange of Native, American, and Mexican cultures that works and prospers; it is a window to the United States' future.

Daniel Stewart is Professor of Entrepreneurship and Director of the Hogan Entrepreneurial Leadership Program at Gonzaga University. He is a member of the Spokane Tribe of Indians. Dan received his Ph.D. (Business) and M.A. (Sociology) from Stanford University. His research appears in leading social science journals such as *American Sociological Review, Organization Science,* and *American Indian Culture and Research Journal.* In addition to his academic activities, Dan is president of Dardan Enterprises, a commercial construction firm, and serves as a board member for various commercial and non-profit organizations.

Kaylynn Sullivan TwoTrees is an Artist/Educator/Activist whose work focuses on reorienting to indigenous mind and regenerating an essential relationship with Earth wisdom. She is currently an Artist in Residence and member of the Leadership Team in the Leadership for Sustainability Masters Program at the University of Vermont and a Whistenton Public Scholar at the Kettering Foundation.

Amy Klemm Verbos, J.D. (University of Wisconsin, 1984), Ph.D. (University of Wisconsin-Milwaukee, 2009), is Assistant Professor of Business Law at the University of Wisconsin-Whitewater. Her work includes publications in the *Journal of Business Ethics, Journal of Management Education, Equality Diversity and Inclusion, Personnel Review, American Indian Culture and Research Journal, Rocky Mountain Law Journal, Human Resource Development Review,* in edited books, and is forthcoming in *Leadership.* Dr. Verbos' research includes relational ethics, Native American ethics, Indigenous inclusion, gender equity, and the Principles of Responsible Management Education. She is an enrolled citizen of the Pokagon Band of Potawatomi.

Index

UNIVERSITY OF WINCHESTER
LIBRARY